city futures

city futures

confronting the crisis of urban development

EDGAR PIETERSE

ZED BOOKS
London & New York

UCT PRESS
Cape Town

City Futures: Confronting the Crisis of Urban Development
was first published in 2008 by:

in southern Africa, UCT Press, an imprint of Juta and Company Limited,
PO Box 14373, Lansdowne, 7779, South Africa
www.uctpress.co.za

in the rest of the world, Zed Books Ltd,
7 Cynthia Street, London N1 9JF, UK
and Room 400, 175 Fifth Avenue, New York NY 10010, USA
www.zedbooks.co.uk

Typeset in Monotype Garamond by illuminati, Grosmont
www.illuminatibooks.co.uk

Cover designed by Andrew Corbett

Printed and bound in the EU by Gutenberg Press Ltd, Malta

Distributed in the USA exclusively by Palgrave Macmillan,
175 Fifth Avenue, New York NY 10010, USA

A catalogue record for this book is available from the British Library
Library of Congress Cataloging in Publication Data available

ISBN 978 1 91989 509 3 (UCT Press)

ISBN 978 1 84277 540 0 Hb (Zed Books)
ISBN 978 1 84277 541 7 Pb (Zed Books)

Contents

Figures and tables

Acknowledgements

This book is written primarily for progressive urban development practitioners within (local) governments, development institutions, NGOs and social movements who are in different ways continuously refining ideas with the aim of advancing a more effective response to the daunting crises unfolding in cities and towns across the world. In light of this, the book cannot be read as an academic guide to the debates, although it does try to bring relevant theoretical perspectives into conversation with pragmatic considerations in order to clarify where we stand and where we need to explore to find more effective responses to the multidimensional knots of injustice in our cities.

The book has been written in a relatively short space of time, but it draws on the experience of twenty years in which I have wrestled with the challenges of urban development and governance in a range of capacities: as activist, trainer, teacher, researcher, public policy manager, consultant and, most recently, scholar. I have been inspired and animated throughout by the tenacity and commitment of the urban activists whose determination is such that they refuse to be defeated by the seemingly insurmountable challenges that come together in cities. I invariably pick up from them something new, often something almost indefinable, that gives me fresh insights into whatever my praxis or obsession may be at a given time. It is impossible to recall all of the generous spirits that I have crossed paths with, and continue to engage with, but I want simply to acknowledge colleagues, comrades and friends whom I have accumulated over the years.

Significant friends and co-conspirators whose ideas and engagements have found their way into many parts of this book are: Askoek Adhikari, Ash Amin, Eve Annecker, Jo Beall, Joel Bolnick, Andrew Boraine, Stephen Boshoff, Owen Crankshaw, Ntone Edjabe, Adi Eindhoven, Alicia Fuentes-Calle, Nthato Gobodo, Graeme Gotz, Gita Govern, Firoz Khan, Christa Kuljian, Barbara Lipietz, Alan Mabin, Neo Muyanga, Mokena Makeka, Dominique Malaquais, Nisa Mammon, Frank Meintjies, Tanner Methvin, Zayd Minty, Luyanda Mpahlwa, Njabulo Ndebele, Sophie Oldfield, Ebrahim Rasool, Kopano Ratele, Alan Roberts, Jennifer Robinson, David Schmidt, Bryan Slingers, AbdouMaliq Simone, Pep Subirós, Barbara Southworth and Vanessa Watson. The Sustainable Cities M.A. class of 2007 at the University of Stellenbosch was a creative inspiration because many of the ideas in the book were tried on them for size; their engagement, alongside that of Mark Swilling, contributed greatly to clarifying my thoughts. Katherine McKenzie offered her valuable time to proofread the full manuscript under very difficult circumstances with generosity and professionalism. I am deeply appreciative. I have also to single out my close friend and intellectual partner in crime, Sue Parnell, who has been a constant source of comradeship, support and encouragement. Zed Books, initially with Robert Molteno and later with Ellen McKinlay and her team, have been incredible in terms of their patience, their professionalism and their commitment.

Family is the constant in our lives that makes it possible to express ourselves. I want to thank all my siblings and their families for their enduring support, and especially my Mom, who is simply always there as the unconditional and proud constant. Ebrahim Rasool, Rosieda Shabodien, Tahrir and Tanwir, thanks for your loving support; and, most importantly, Mirjam van Donk and Rafael Zukile Pieterse, thanks for the home and fun where I'm allowed to be me.

Finally, writing ebbs and flows to a soundtrack, and the one carrying this book afloat includes brilliant music by: Tony Allen, MV Bill, the Branford Marsalis Quartet, Celso Fonseca, Common, Dave Matthews, Marisa Monte, Cassandra Wilson, Roots Manuva, Tom Waits, Lekou Wanza, Richard Bona and Toto, Lizz Wright, U-Cef.

For Rafael & Mirjam

I

Introduction:

deciphering city futures

With cities, it is as with dreams: everything imaginable can be dreamed, but even the most unexpected dream is a rebus that conceals a desire, or, its reverse, a fear. Cities, like dreams, are made up of desires and fears, even if the thread of their discourse is secret, their rules are absurd, their perspectives deceitful, and everything conceals something else.[1]

Nothing about cities in the twenty-first century is insignificant; the stakes are always high in pinning down what cities are, in thinking about what to do with cities and in acting on/in/through the city, especially if one wants to bring to life more liberating and just futures. For this reason it is extremely difficult to find a conceptual path that cuts through the vicissitudes of the city without losing one's way in blind alleys and dead ends. Before I delve into what will come in the following chapters it is opportune to render explicit the coordinates that anchor the conceptual lens I use in finding my way through the maze of competing perspectives and experiences of the contemporary city.

In very broad terms the literature on the contemporary city in the global South[2] can be divided between those who take an apocalyptic view and those who display an irrepressible optimism about the possibility of solving the myriad problems that beset such cities. For instance, *Planet of Slums* by the prolific urbanist Mike Davis provides a relentless catalogue of the utterly devastating conditions that characterize the daily lives of the majority of the world's urban dwellers. At the end of this book one is left emotionally devastated but also virtually incapacitated because on every conceivable front of potential change, one encounters the superior cunning of an oppressive system that will simply reinvent the conditions of exploitation. The Davis book foresees an interminable state of exploitation as it awaits the 'future of human solidarity [which] depends upon the militant refusal of the new urban poor to accept their terminal marginality within global capitalism'.[3] At this end of the spectrum, scholars and policy activists insist that without addressing the framing conditions of the global economy it is not possible to solve urban poverty.

The register of urban implosion finds it difficult not merely to see victims – victims of corrupt governments (politicians and bureaucrats); victims of unscrupulous private firms that cherry-pick profitable services whilst leaving the poor to fend for themselves; victims of patronizing NGOs that neutralize militant resistance through their ameliorative 'good' works; victims of deeply entrenched cultural affiliations that get mobilized to exploit and abuse those considered inferior in terms of race, ethnicity and caste whilst allowing the real profiteers to get away with the loot; victims of (extreme) weather conditions due to bad locations in the city, which in turn link back to being powerless. In the fulcrum of compounded victimhood, it is almost impossible to imagine possibilities of resistance, liberation and empowerment. In contradistinction, scholars like Malcolm Jack treat the urban poor like a 'blank figure' with little awareness or reference to the conditions that must be endured while mainstream institutions get their act together and pursue a rational policy agenda that will, incrementally, fix the conditions of urban poverty bit by bit.[4] This is maybe an unreasonable depiction of conventional apolitical policy-prescriptive studies, but it seems to me that unreflexive policy prescription in the wake of the impasse in development studies – or, more accurately, when development studies lost its innocence – is deeply problematic, for it reinforces a confidence among the powerful that has profound disempowering effects.[5]

There is a third seam of analysis that attempts to work through the experiences and 'everyday practices' of the urban majority who draw

the short end of the stick in contemporary cities. These commenta-
tors draw attention to the pervasive system of informalization – that
is, partially outside of formal economies, conventional governance
systems and enumerated areas – that flows from the unjust structures
of opportunity in cities. However, instead of reading only marginalization and exclusion from the urban, these writers also point to the
ways in which marginalization can be read differently as a zone of
possibility and autonomy in various interstices of the city, even if
in circumscribed ways.[6] I do not want to get into the merits of this
approach, but simply want to draw attention to the fact that unless
the complex, dynamic, highly improvising and generative actions
of the urban poor are acknowledged and explored, it is foolish to
come to conclusions about what is going on in a city, or what may
or may not work, either from an insurrectionary perspective or from
a 'policy-fix' approach.

The importance of the informal register in reading the city is that
it compels one to take a more provisional approach before one pro-
nounces on either what is going on, or what must be done to improve
the quality of life and freedom in the city. For, as AbdouMaliq
Simone reminds us:

> Cities are densities of stories, passions, hurts, revenge, aspiration, avoid-
> ance, deflection, and complicity. As such, residents must be able to
> conceive of a space sufficiently bounded so as to consolidate disparate
> energies and make things of scale happen. But at the same time, they
> must conceive of a fractured space sufficiently large enough through
> which dangerous feelings can dissipate or be steered away. Urban
> residents are thus concerned about what kinds of games, instruments,
> languages, sight lines, constructions, and objects can be put in play in
> order to anticipate new alignments of social initiatives and resources,
> and thus capacity.[7]

Thus, today (if ever) it is simply inconceivable to approach or
move through the city and its futures with irrevocable certainty
about what is going on or what is needed to make the place better.
Conceptual analysis and policy prescription must move with great
care and reflexivity.[8] Does this mean that one cannot perceive and
engage with what are surely blatant deployments of dominating power
over those with little material or political resources? Of course not;

it remains perfectly possible and essential to uncover the multiple and complex circuitries of power in the city, but unfortunately this is unlikely to render a simple story line of domineering power where it is clear-cut who the perpetrators and victims are. This takes me on to another set of coordinates that shape the approach of the book.

Power and complexity

It is crucial to appreciate the constitutive nature of power and complexity in the city. Any analysis of urban conditions and future prospects must come to terms with the dimensions of complexity and the ways in which it is sutured by various dynamics of power. This opens the door, conceptually, to two central ideas of the book: *radical incrementalism* and *recursive political empowerment*. But first a few comments of clarification on the intertwined ideas of complexity and power, and particularly the tension wire that runs between these dynamics and that animates much in the contemporary city.

Following the work of anthropologist Emery Roe, one can link complexity to the reality of contingency which gives rise to incessant uncertainties and surprises in most development contexts. Of course such uncertainties coexist with structural factors that reproduce uneven spatial development patterns, but such factors do not explain or predetermine the fate of development ambitions and interventions. According to Roe, development issues are fundamentally 'highly uncertain and complex [because] many, if not most, parties to these issues, including the experts, are in the grip of many unknowns, frequent surprise, and little agreement, where few involved know what really is in their best long-run interests, and where almost everyone is playing it by ear – and this includes the so-called power brokers.'[9] In more recent times complexity theory as a philosophical stream has also been deployed to capture the interactions of various physical, social, economic, political, ecological and cultural systems in urban spaces, producing an infinite number of unpredictable dynamics. Thus, for urbanist David Byrne, the city must be approached and explored as a fundamentally emergent and therefore open-ended reality:

> Cities are plainly dissipative complex systems with emergent properties and evolutionary history. The identification of cities as dissipative systems matters a great deal because it describes the relationship between

urban places, the 'unnatural' location of contemporary life within a
'built' environment and the natural systems of this planet. Cities are
indeed complex systems but complex systems embedded within both
the complex system of global economic and cultural relations, and the
complex systems which compose the natural world.[10]

What this mouthful suggests is that there are always so many variables
at play in how cities function, unfold and incessantly become something different; it is important to assume a constitutive complexity,
heightened by the rapidity of change in a globalized world, as central
to the rebus character of cities.

On the other hand it is also fair to say that even if we are to
appreciate the significance of complexity, uncertainty, surprise and
therefore open-ended futures, or at least malleable futures, we cannot
deny that power is at the heart of city development, because governance boils down to questions of control over decision-making about
how resources are used in a sea of competing and different interests.
Fortunately our thinking about power has evolved beyond mere
notions of 'who benefits?', 'who is getting exploited?', 'how badly
are they exploited?', to understanding the dynamic, capillary and
decentred nature of circuits of power, which are always unstable and
vulnerable to resistance and transformation.[11] In response to Roe, and
taking on board the insights about complexity, anthropologist Donald
Moore offers a useful multifaceted approach to power:

> Instead of simply mapping typologies of power [as Roe does], alterna-
> tive perspectives could emphasize the practices through which power
> operates, the symbolic and material effects power produces, and its
> performance. In feminist cultural critic Judith Butler's terms: 'Perfor-
> mativity describes this relation of being implicated in that which one
> opposes, this turning of power against itself to reproduce alternative
> modalities of power, to establish a kind of political contestation that is
> not a "pure" opposition, a "transcendence" of contemporary relations
> of power, but a difficult labor of forging a future from resources
> inevitably impure.'[12]

The reason I find these two lenses – complexity and power – useful
is because they allow one to respond to the existing mainstream
literature and more critical conceptual approaches to cities and begin
to build something akin to a bridge between them. The complexity

lens allows us to address the technical, technocratic and managerialist discourses and imperatives characteristic of the various literatures in the domain of urban management. Thus, Chapters 3 and 4 start with a critical engagement with mainstream policy discourses that seek to address the challenges of intensifying urbanization with respect to the managerial and technical complexity of the issues at stake. At the same time, this book stresses that technical solutions are often oblivious to power dynamics and by default are in fact profoundly political in their effects – a danger that is ever present as progressive-sounding urban policies continue to produce or perpetuate unjust and inequitable urban outcomes.

Radical incrementalism

The existential core of urbanism is the desire for *radical change* to bring all the good implied in the original utopian association of 'the city'.[13] This radical impulse stands in contrast to the necessary prudence and constraints of *incremental change*, which is the only way of intervening in conditions of profound complexity and entrenched power dynamics embedded in capitalist modernities.

We know that the current scale of human suffering and violence that flow from the profoundly unequal distribution of resources and opportunity is fundamentally inhumane and intolerable. Yet we also know that we cannot wish into existence an overnight revolution that will make everything all right in the world. At the same time it seems futile simply to work away at creating the right conditions for insurrectionary revolutions that will eventually bring to life a large-scale 'militant refusal' by the world's urban multitudes, as intimated by Mike Davis. This leaves one with bringing change into the world through more discrete avenues: surreptitious, sometimes overt, and multiple small revolutions that at unanticipated and unexpected moments galvanize into deeper ruptures that accelerate tectonic shifts of the underlying logics of domination and what is considered possible. Radical incrementalism is a disposition and sensibility that believes in deliberate actions of social transformation but through a multiplicity of processes and imaginations, none of which assumes or asserts a primary significance over other struggles. This position may not resolve the existential struggle of urbanism, but it provides a means to confront the struggle and perpetually work one's way through it, stumbling across what works and what does not. Stuart Hall captured this sensibility with great acuity: 'are we not all, in different ways, and through different conceptual spaces ... desperately trying to understand what making an ethical political choice and taking a political position in a necessarily open and contingent political field is like, what sort of "politics" it adds up to?'[14] This book takes this sensibility of ethical searching into the domain of urban change and renewal. Holding this sensibility in mind, I explore what I mean by recursive political empowerment.

Recursive political empowerment

Transformative change in cities cannot be bestowed by a (benign) state; nor can it take root simply as a consequence of good policy plus political will (whatever this overused and underspecified notion may mean). Transformative urban change that leads to the enhancement of 'capabilities' of the poor and abandoned requires agency by these very same constituencies, agency ideally inserted into a multidirectional meshwork of institutions and discourses that frame the functioning and reproduction of urban systems. However, the mobilization of these constituencies is not at all a straightforward matter, because 'the poor' and 'the abandoned' are never cohesive, or coherent, or homogenous in any way. Complex and shifting identities and group-based associations, embedded in dynamic cultural processes, render the urban majorities inherently fragmented and contested. Furthermore, neighbourhoods and associational circuits where the urban poor are concentrated are typically stratified by deep power differentials between those who control and channel resources in and out of these areas and those rendered dependent on such gatekeeping.

Engaging with these multilayered realities requires a degree of awareness and a (personal) decision to participate in structures and processes that can lead to an improvement in one's lot. Significantly, people's sense of possibility is closely tied to culturally shaped assessments of opportunities and threats associated with participation. Such calculations, in turn, are intertwined with a sense of being and self in relation to place and particular communities.[15] Thus, a

viable notion of empowerment of the poor requires an appreciation that empowerment is fundamentally an individual process that
deepens with time if individual efforts are consciously embedded in
more collective forms of solidarity and mutual empowerment. The
practice of Shack/Slum Dwellers International (SDI), explored in
Chapters 3 and 6, illustrates this effectively. SDI explicitly seeks to
build autonomy from the state and informal power brokers, whilst
socializing their members into an alternative normative framework,
which in turn becomes the basis of mobilization and legitimacy in
their work.

Framing propositions

On the basis of these conceptual coordinates, the book is premissed
on a number of propositions. First, in dealing with the myriad problems associated with urban development, the central problematic that
must be addressed is urban inequality. This focus allows one to keep
in view the ways in which the framing conditions of the increasingly integrated global economic system places severe limits on the
radicalism of urban interventions and experiments. The economic
vested interests that tie together urban elites across societal and
national cleavages make it almost impossible to propose, let alone
pursue with any modicum of success, alternative economic systems
and initiatives.[16] Yet, unless one is able to address and systematically reverse urban inequalities, the prospects of creating more just,
inclusive and vibrant cities are bleak. Therefore, on the back of the
more overtly 'moral' turn in global development forums and circuits
(e.g. the Millennium Development Summit of 2000, which spawned
the MDGs for 2015), there is an opportunity to use the (diversionary)
focus on urban poverty to make linkages to the more fundamental
conditions driving inequality that fall along various faultlines: class,
race, ethnicity, caste, location, religion, ability, gender, sexual preference, age, and so on. This can become a key strategic plank in
progressive coalitions and networks mobilizing to remake cities in
the global South.

Second, particular 'network infrastructures' are privileged at the
moment to create favourable conditions for economic productivity
and competitiveness. These are infrastructures that facilitate the rapid

movements of goods and services as cities are pushed to reinvent themselves as magnets for investment in a globalizing world. In the logic of pursuing these particular infrastructures, the location and infrastructure needs of the poor take a back seat to what the city may need to become competitive, and, more recently, 'creative'. As Stephen Graham and Simon Marvin demonstrate in their authoritative overview, network infrastructure pressures tend to further skew public resource allocations and reinforce the marginalization of the urban poor at different scales. The point about this trend is that in the discourses surrounding the need for increased investment in 'connectivity infrastructures', spaces open up to demonstrate how most urban infrastructures are indeed indispensable but also fundamentally public goods because of their functions in satisfying the full gamut of human rights. In other words, spaces of counter-discursive strategies become possible as the right to sustainable livelihood infrastructures becomes the basis for more critical political campaigns that assert the general 'right to the city' over the sectional interests of urban elites to live in enclaves and profit indiscriminately off, essentially, public investments.

Third, the phenomenology and practices of 'the everyday' or 'the ordinary' must be the touchstone of radical imaginings and interventions. Everyday realities are most compellingly captured in artistic, literary and anthropological accounts because these registers are most attuned to the intimate textures of socialities forged in the midst of very difficult and painful circumstances, as meticulously captured by Mike Davis in *Planet of Slums*. Social interactions and identity constructive dynamics are not simple or easy narratives. Ben Okri's classic novel *Dangerous Love*, set in a slum in Lagos during the civil war of 1970s' Nigeria, reminds one of the desires and pleasures that can coexist in even the most abject of conditions; and so do the philosophical musings of Alphonso Lingis as he rekindles the affective sensualities of desire in the *favelas* of Rio and slums in Manila, among many other 'desperate' places.[17] One also gets a glimpse of the affective effects of popular music in the pulsating scenes of the film *City of God*, as kids from the slum find rapturous ecstasy in the musky, sweaty, sweltering dancehalls of the *favela*. This is not to romanticize the difficulties and brutalities of grinding poverty and persistent terror, but rather to recuperate the constitutive humanity and, by extension, generative powers of the ordinary.[18] For policy purposes it is worth remembering that literary registers that turn our gaze to the informal, the interior and the interstitial, away from the grand swells of exploitation, offer crucial insight and guidance into how one can deploy an awareness and respect for the ordinary in seeking to transform the city.

Fourth, urbanists serious about transformative change must be able to work dextrously with a wide array of policy tools and instruments. Dexterity comes in handy because urban change is massaged at a multiplicity of pressure points across the city and its institutional scaffolding. Public resources are typically organized into sectoral services such as water, sanitation, transportation, roads, electricity, housing, and so forth. Traditionally these services are underpinned by vast specialist knowledge rooted in particular modernist disciplines. During the past three decades, it became evident that urban services need to be planned and deployed in a more coordinated fashion to improve outcomes and, as a consequence, these disciplinary boundaries have been pushed to become more porous. Policy frameworks such as Local Agenda 21, local economic development strategies, livelihoods approaches and the like, generally rest on a multi-sectoral approach, stressing the interdependencies and linkages between services.

More recently it has also become clearer that the spatial scale at which a service is delivered matters a great deal for how one conceptualizes and operationalizes inter-sectoral coordination and integration. For example, sanitation services depend on the nature and scope of water catchment dynamics at regional scales that extend well beyond the boundaries of a city. At the same time, the delivery of sanitation-related services at a household scale must be closely linked to the planning and delivery of a set of services that constitute a local area, amenable to neighbourhood or quarter development. What may constitute a progressive set of policies at a regional scale related to the political economy of water catchments and management may not coincide with what is progressive at a neighbourhood scale. Consequently, one has always to have one's strategic wits about oneself so as to avoid grave strategic errors in promoting what may seem to be a very principled and morally defensible policy at one scale, but simultaneously disempowering at another scale of organization and struggle.

Fifth, all forms of urban imagination and intervention are inherently political and therefore prone to critique and mobilization. However, if various dimensions of urban imaginaries and practices are not effectively articulated, possibilities of transformation dissipate into the ether. The first step in understanding the possibilities of *strategic articulation* is to recognize the ways in which the urban polity is sliced into various overlapping and mutually implicated institutional sites of engagement and contestation. In any urban polity the following five generic sites of politics can be identified: (1) representative political forums, such as local government councils, the executive arm of the local authority and various avenues for more direct participation by citizens in structures such as ward committees, district public assemblies, and so on; (2) neo-corporatist political mechanisms that comprise representative organizations, typically the government, the private sector, trade unions and, occasionally, community-based organizations (i.e. stakeholders) focused on macro-policy deliberation, coordination and consensus – these structures are less widespread but growing in importance under the policy imperatives of 'partnerships' and 'strategic planning'; (3) direct action or mobilization by social movements against state policies or to advance specific political demands for response or incorporation into government programmes and/or in relation to business actions or influence; (4) the politics of development practice – grassroots engagement in social, environmental and economic development projects to benefit targeted groups and/or areas; and (5) symbolic political contestation as expressed through discursive exchange and projection in the public sphere.[19] These are obviously only conceptual distinctions. In gritty real-life conditions these institutional domains are intimately connected, and often an action in one institutional arena can trigger responses in another. I continuously return to this model, which provides the political thread of the book.

The second step in grasping the possibilities of strategic articulation is to adopt a more nuanced approach to reading urban politics as expressed in competing discourses, diverse and divergent urban

actors, networks and coalitions, and, most importantly, the governance cultures within which these actors and associated discourses
are embedded. The recent work of Patsy Healey is most instructive in this regard. Her model of the dimensions of governance
suggests that there are three dimensions to local (political) power
dynamics. In the first instance, specific episodes (e.g. attracting a
particular high-profile event, or addressing a particular basic service
need like sanitation services, or dealing with street children) tend
to structure and drive political attention. As these episodes unfold,
working their way to a plan, a programme, a project/business plan
with an attendant budget, one can identify the actors involved (and
marginalized), the strategies they deploy in seeking to secure their
interests; all of which may not be that predictable, because informal
agreements and deals may influence how politicians, or officials for
that matter, act on a specific issue. In addition, the way these issues
are framed, talked about and relayed – discursive formations – is
critical to understand what is being included/excluded from debates
and decision-making. What's more, the issues addressed in an episode
are always dealt with in specific institutional sites, which are associated with particular 'rules of the game' that must be adhered to.
Indeed, if one reflects on the five political domains listed above (as
well as their interfaces), clearly very different kinds of politics get
mobilized and driven in different institutional sites. Crucially, how
issues are debated, dealt with, resolved or not, is informed by the
deeply embedded governance culture of a locality or region. In a
governance culture actors typically know what they can and cannot
say; they know when to play to the media gallery and when not
to; they know how to speak for particular interests without saying
they are speaking for sectional interests; and so on. Again, these
cultures tend to be highly particular in each municipality and also
in different provinces or states depending on the larger balance of
forces and discursive parameters in the public sphere. Clearly, one
cannot explore strategic political articulation in the absence of a
detailed enough map along the vectors intimated in this governance
model (see Table 1.1).[20]

Only when urban actors are able to position their politics within
a framework mapped across the various dimensions of the urban

TABLE 1.1 Dimensions of governance

Level	Dimension
Specific episodes	• Actors: roles, strategies and interests • Arenas: institutional sites • Settings and interactive practices: communicative repertoires
Governance processes through which bias is mobilized	• Networks and coalitions • Stakeholder selection processes • Discourses: framing issues, problems, solutions, etc. • Practices: routines and repertoires for acting • Specification of laws, formal competences and resource flow principles
Governance cultures	• Range of accepted modes of governance • Range of embedded cultural values • Formal and informal structures for policing discourses and practices

polity, and grounded in a rigorous understanding of the specificities of the governance culture they seek to influence, does it become possible to foster a politics of radical incrementalism and recursive empowerment.

There is no single answer to the global challenge of urban justice, so sorely lacking in every crevice of the world's cities. There is no magic bullet that can solve the multiple and interwoven dimensions of brutalization and exclusion that work so contemptuously in most cities. All we have is a way of 'walking'/traversing the city, which in turn immediately changes shape as one moves through its folds and shadows, trying to figure out what combination of strategies and tactics can be summoned to thicken the energies for transformation and renewal.

Outline of the book

In view of this conceptual underpinning of the book, the logic of the chapters is the following. First of all I summarize the most recent urbanization trends data, disaggregated by regions of the global South. This is important because it alerts readers not only to the scale and urgency of the issues involved but also to the vastly different settings that predominate in various parts of the world. This constitutive heterogeneity is an important reference throughout the book. Second, the book engages with the two most high-profile mainstream policy responses – the shelter for all and good urban governance campaigns – championed by international development bodies such as UN–Habitat, the World Bank and Cities Alliance. In the two chapters devoted to this I highlight the main tenets of these initiatives and offer a critique of them in order to lay the basis for an alternative perspective that works with what is valuable in the mainstream consensus but also seeks to supplant it with a more robust argument. The central premiss of the critique is that mainstream urban development policies tend to depoliticize urban development policy objectives and instruments, which paradoxically makes it even harder to truly advance the normative ambitions of the 1996 Habitat Agenda, the wellspring of the two campaigns for urban reform. Thus the central chapter offers a theoretical exposition of the kind of politics – that is, radical democratic – that is required as a foundation for the emergence of sustainable lives and livelihoods. Chapter 5 offers a fleshed out argument of the five domains of political practice mentioned before, but it also serves as a foundation for the second half of the book, which is in a more propositional register.

In Chapter 6, the book takes a brief detour to foreground insurgent practices and dynamics in the city. Given the focus of this chapter, and its destabilizing function in relation to the cleaner rational form of argument in chapters 5, 7 and 8, it purposefully takes on a different tone. The purpose is to foreground the indeterminacy of everyday life – usually missed – of particularly the poor, as expressed through their stubborn appropriation of the city for the purposes of survival and reproducing, often highly precarious, livelihoods. Given the inordinate difficulty academic and policy discourses have with capturing the rich phenomenology of the everyday, I draw on examples from literature and cultural practices, to illuminate the lived realities of the city. Without suggesting any possibility of a linear instrumental appropriation of these dynamics for transformative urban development policy, the purpose of this chapter is to remind us of the undercurrent of ordinary inventiveness that necessarily shadows the efforts of the urban poor to keep limb, life and the aspirations of a better future alive.

Chapter 7 takes on a more conventional procedural logic to specify more plainly the central elements of my reading of an alternative urban development framework. A conceptual model is presented which draws attention to the relationship between radical democracy and levers for systemic change towards more sustainable and resilient urban patterns. The chapter offers a set of concrete tools for networks and coalitions of urban radicals to work at the border zones of mainstream policy discourses but decidedly against the grain to show up limits and contradictions, with an eye on specifying more effective alternatives amenable to being scaled up in the actions of local states, civil society organizations and sections of the business community that are serious about contributing to more inclusive, sustainable and equitable city futures. The final chapter attempts to get even more practical and provides a policy framework to address urban poverty in a multidimensional framework, and cognizant of the larger, globalized political economic forces that drive rising levels of inter- and intra-regional inequality. The chapter concludes with a hypothetical exploration of how the various elements of the book's overall argument come together in the idea of 'tipping points': that is, unique, city-specific interventions that are rich in cultural resonance and effectively address the systemic drivers of a profoundly stubborn problem within a particular city. It is my belief that if progressives adopt a more proactive, forward-looking and creative approach to the rich potentiality of our cities across the global South, the prospect of city futures where the right to the city is the norm stops simply being a dream.

2

Urbanization trends

and implications

This chapter seeks to provide a particular perspective on the complex, uneven and often confusing dynamics of urbanization as it plays out in different parts of the South. A plethora of books and magazine articles on the crossing of a 'majority urban world' threshold in 2008 have made their appearance in the recent period, which reduces the need for detailed statistical presentation of the scale, pace, direction and differential impact of urbanization across the world. Although I draw on some of the urbanization trends data of the United Nations, I mainly aim to provide a reading, an interpretation, of what is unfolding to lay the basis for the discussions that follow in the rest of the book. The aim is not to provide a comprehensive review of urbanization statistics; David Satterthwaite, whose work is seminal in this regard, does this effectively.[1] The core argument is that we are witnessing the second wave of urbanization – in contrast to the first wave that took place in Europe and North America between 1750 and 1950. The current wave is taking place within a particular geopolitical and economic moment in the history of humanity, which presents daunting pressures and decisions for urban citizens and especially activists, leaders and managers as they figure out how to cope and flourish.

The most useful label (albeit one open to a wide range of interpretations) for the contemporary political economy of territorial development (at various interlinked scales – local, sub-national, national, regional, global) is of course globalization. As a dense constellation of various economic, political, social, cultural and ecological processes, globalization drives particular economic and spatial dynamics in cities and towns across the world. On the economic side, globalization imperatives for market access and asymmetrical integration hold serious implications for the territorial infrastructural imperatives of urban development, especially as the bulk of economic value-added comes from service sectors that are largely knowledge-intensive. Thus, in most cities and towns of the South, public decision-makers are forced to address both economic and social infrastructural imperatives from a very limited and constrained fiscus and invariably find themselves in the invidious position of having to make trade-offs, or at best sequencing decisions, about where public resources will be invested. It is this choice, or trade-off, that I want to delve into in this chapter by drawing on the work of Stephen Graham and Simon Marvin, who trace and theorize the rising importance of 'splintered network infrastructures'.[2]

Globalization also seems to induce particular spatial dynamics in the evolution and management of urban territories and systems. In particular, greater spatial segregation and often exclusion of the urban poor are in evidence as cities jostle to become 'world class' and 'globally connected', at least for the enclaves of professional knowledge workers who reside there. The starkest expression of urban division and exclusion is the dramatic rise in slums in the global South over the past three decades. It is also this feature of the contemporary condition that is receiving the most policy attention. I therefore spend some time going over this literature in order to tease out where we stand in the global policy debate about the relationship (or trade-offs) between investing and managing economic versus social reproduction and public goods infrastructures. Through this review it becomes apparent that most local governments in the South are caught in a terrible bind of contradictory policy imperatives, which create fertile ground for powerful vested interests in cities, which are either tied into globalized circuits of capital or benefit from the absence of regulation and equity within zones of informal exclusion, to become even more entrenched.

Dimensions of the second wave of urbanization

In the *State of the World Population 2007*, the population division of the United Nations introduces a useful lens with which to think about the significance and scale of contemporary urbanization.[3] It is worthwhile quoting the report at some length because of its foundational value for the discussion that follows:

> The first urbanization wave took place in North America and Europe over two centuries, from 1750 to 1950: an increase from 10 to 52 per cent urban and from 15 to 423 million urbanites. In the second wave of urbanization, in the less developed regions, the number of urbanites will go from 309 million in 1950 to 3.9 billion in 2030. In those 80 years, these countries will change from 18 per cent to some 56 per cent urban.
>
> At the beginning of the 20th century, the now developed regions had more than twice as many urban dwellers as the less developed (150 million to 70 million). Despite much lower levels of urbanization, the developing countries now have 2.6 times as many urban dwellers as the developed regions (2.3 billion to 0.9 billion). This gap will widen quickly in the next few decades.
>
> At the world level, the 20th century saw an increase from 220 million urbanites in 1900 to 2.84 billion in 2000. The present century will match this absolute increase in about four decades. Developing regions as a whole will account for 93 per cent of this growth, Asia and Africa for over 80 per cent.
>
> Between 2000 and 2030, Asia's urban population will increase from 1.36 billion to 2.64 billion, Africa's from 294 million to 742 million, and that of Latin America and the Caribbean from 394 million to 609 million. As a result of these shifts, developing countries will have 80 per cent of the world's urban population in 2030. By then, Africa and Asia will include almost seven out of every ten urban inhabitants in the world.[4]

To achieve a perspective on the magnitude of these shifts, it is revealing to historicize the declining time needed for one billion urban dwellers to be added to the total (Table 2.1).

The vast bulk of the new urban dwellers that swelled the numbers from the 1960s onwards have been in developing countries. Table 2.2

TABLE 2.1 The declining time needed for 1 billion additional urban dwellers[5]

World's total urban population	Time taken
0–1 billion	10,000 years (c. 8000 BCE–1960)
1–2 billion	25 years (1960–1985)
2–3 billion	18 years (1985–2003)
3–4 billion	15 years (2003–2018)

TABLE 2.2 Urban population by region, 1950–2000, with projection for 2010 (million inhabitants)[6]

Region	1950	1970	1990	2000	2010
Africa	33	85	203	294	408
Asia	234	485	1,011	1,363	1,755
Latin America and Caribbean	70	163	315	394	474
Europe	277	411	509	522	529
North America	110	171	214	249	284
Oceania	8	14	19	22	25
World	732	1,329	2,271	2,845	3,475

provides a more precise breakdown of these shifts and captures how the growth rates in Africa and Asia in particular are very significant and will remain so, according to United Nations projections, until 2030.

The big leaps in urban populations to which it is worth drawing attention occur from the 1970s onwards. This is highly significant because the world economy also deepened the long-term process of profound restructuring that today we refer to in shorthand as globalization. As will become clear in a moment, globalization processes were underpinned by profound technological shifts – computerization

– that have far-reaching territorial implications. Nation-states become less central to economic coordination and regulation and both supra-national and sub-national scales of economic activity and regulation rise in importance. Furthermore, economic activity, especially high value-added activities, becomes more and more dependent on information and knowledge management – that is, intangible services that do not require an agricultural or manufacturing industrial base. Moreover, agricultural and manufacturing activities that succeed in making their production and distribution processes more mechanized, computerized and knowledge-driven (e.g. informed by specialized information about market segments to ensure higher prices for tailored products) survive in the new economic context. Those countries and localities that do not have access to investment capital, appropriately skilled workers, good communications and transportation links to worldwide markets face profound economic marginalization and even obsolescence.

Longitudinal data demonstrate that agricultural activity (in contradistinction to manufacturing and services) has been contributing less than 30 per cent of GDP in developing countries since 1965 and plummeted further to 11 per cent by 2005.[7] This is highly significant given that the majority of populations in Asia and Africa will be in rural areas until at least 2025.[8] In other words, economic opportunities are only likely to grow in urban areas, except where rural economies are able to reposition into service activities that accompany tourism and high-value agroprocessing. This trend has existed for some time, which explains much of the dramatic migration of rural populations to urban areas – jobs and the hope of better future prospects are largely only available in urban areas.

The flipside of this picture is that manufacturing and services now contribute 90 per cent of GDP in most developing countries. Even in sub-Saharan Africa, which is only 39 per cent urbanized, 89 per cent of GDP comes from industry and services.[9] However, the economic nature of industry/manufacturing and services has dramatically changed over the past three decades. In the case of manufacturing, the rise of ever more sophisticated machines that could exploit technological breakthroughs in computer chip miniaturization, whilst exponentially increasing processing capacity and dropping in cost, meant that the industrial production process could be radically transformed to move away from standardized mass products to a highly variegated output that could tailor-make products for various niche markets; a process that is referred to as flexible specialization, characteristic of the post-Fordist production system. In this context, those manufacturing firms that were able to capture wealthy consumers by producing design-intensive niche products succeeded. What this shift involved, of course, was a devastating impact on labour. On the one hand, fewer workers were needed, resulting in massive lay-offs of semi-skilled and unskilled workers. Also, those who could retain their jobs had to become a lot more skilled and expert in running more complex, adaptive and rapidly changing production systems. As a result, a new international division of labour (NIDL) began to emerge in the 1970s.

> The NIDL refer to a spatial division of labour at the global scale.... Under the OIDL [old international division of labour], the global periphery was seen and theorized as the provider of many goods and raw materials for processing in 'core' countries in Western Europe and North America. In exchange for these materials, the periphery received finished goods manufactured in the core. The economic activities in the global core and periphery are changing under the development of the new international division of labour. A process of vertical uncoupling, subdivision, and/or subcontracting of production results in the periphery developing low-skilled, standardized operations such as manufacturing assembly or routine data entry, while the global core retains high skilled knowledge- or technology-intensive industry and occupations. Through deskilling of labour, and the functional and physical separation of various tasks in the corporation, this process creates 'roles' for places in the world economy.[10]

The NIDL is usefully illustrated by Nike's worldwide production system in which the high value-added activities remain in the North and low-wage activities are undertaken in the South. But even in the South there is further differentiation between countries that handle subcontracting relations with factories where the actual assembly takes place. In the case of Nike, design aspects that go into the conceptualization of the shoe take place in the USA; the fostering of markets through extremely expensive advertising campaigns premised on customer-based research remains in the USA;

the management of moving of the goods to the point of assembly
and the finished products to the retail outlets in the North and
middle income countries, are handled by countries such as Taiwan
and Korea. The actual assembly takes place in two categories of
countries: high-end products that require higher levels of skill in
Taiwan and Korea; low-end product assembly in China, Indonesia
and Vietnam.[11] In this geographically stretched production and retail
system, all of the high-value activities – essentially services – remain
in the North, and routine manufacturing assembly functions are
performed in developing countries where the cities structure their
infrastructure investments and regulatory systems to capture this
kind of economic activity.

It is vital to appreciate that only a section of developing countries
were able to build their economies on the basis of these structural
economic shifts, namely the newly industrialized countries (NICs),
also known as the Asian Tigers. The skewed pattern is reflected in
various indicators, but let us simply focus on shares of world exports
given the importance of vigorous trade relations in maintaining an
economic foothold. In 1980, East Asia and the Pacific accounted for
about a 3 per cent share of world exports and this had increased to
9 per cent by 2002. However, over this period sub-Saharan Africa
declined from a 3 per cent share of world trade (the level of East
Asia) to 0.7 per cent![12] Territorially, what happened in the developing
countries that did participate in the NIDL is striking. Most of the
NICs introduced policies to establish enclaves of production – export
processing zones – where the conventional regimes of taxation and
labour regulation were suspended. Furthermore, high-quality transportation, logistics and other infrastructures would be provided tax
free (at least for the initial years) in order to lure investors.[13] These
initiatives became the anchor points for an export-oriented indus-
trialization model that underpins the dramatic growth of Southeast
Asian countries since the late 1960s. The developmental model of
the NICs was to subsidize the production activities of transnational
corporations (TNCs), whilst investing heavily in education so that
they could steadily monopolize skilled manufacturing off a low
wage base. In this way, as the ICT revolution gained pace, they
became more and more pivotal to globalized production chains. In

urban management terms what this meant was major investments in economic infrastructure to secure and retain the manufacturing activities of TNCs. In this division of economic activity, the North retained coordination, product design and marketing functions, which in turn became more and more profitable because competitiveness depends increasingly on data and knowledge management functions. This brings me to a brief discussion on the rise of service sectors over the last three decades as the world absorbed a further 2 billion urban dwellers.

By the late 1990s, the shares of agriculture, manufactures/industry, and services were 6 per cent, 36 per cent and 58 per cent, respectively.[14] Typical economic activities that make up services are: financial services, insurance, real estate, legal services, media and communications (especially advertising), tourism, transportation, research and development or knowledge production, and so forth. In an increasingly globalized production system, the coordination functions of TNCs are very important because they ensure optimal efficiency in terms of tailoring products to ever changing specialized demand from ever growing market segments. Thus, the greatest economic value accrues to highly skilled, specialized activities that make up the service industry. Saskia Sassen has been tracing the spatial/territorial significance of particular global cities that attract and concentrate the most lucrative and specialist economic services that the globe-spanning web of TNCs have relied on since the early 1990s. In her work she demonstrates that these various knowledge-driven services, paradoxically in a wired world, depend on close proximity and territorial concentration to perform optimally.[15] In other words, there are very particular locational factors that inform the decisions of these companies. In her reading, tellingly, there are no primary global cities in the South. However, what is striking is that many cities in the South and North (bypassed by the high-end services circuit) aspire to become global cities and will do just about anything to achieve that status. In other words, there is profound status and prestige associated with being a hub for high-end knowledge-intensive firms, especially in the financial services sector.

Over the past forty years, when 2 billion urban dwellers were added to the global total, the economic function of urban territories has undergone a profound change. This has made it possible for some places to achieve unimaginable levels of prosperity while the majority of urban settlements have become profoundly economically marginalized. Furthermore, even those places that have benefited have become increasingly unequal and now manifest very profound internal barriers between the economically active and the excluded.[16] Those cities and towns that aspire to be 'globally competitive' are compelled to accept that economic success requires major sacrifices and interminable inequality. This is a very large claim; to substantiate it, I want to draw on the pathbreaking work of Stephen Graham and Simon Marvin, who unpack the infrastructural underpinnings of the emergent global economic system, anchored as it is in urban territories.

Splintered network infrastructures

The argument developed by Graham and Marvin starts off with the observation that towards the tail end of the first wave of urbanization in the early twentieth century, European and North American cities (and to a significant degree Japanese cities as well) sought to roll out vast technological infrastructure to ensure access to water, power and communications, as well as urban highways. From the 1930s onwards, emphasis fell on the receding of 'technological networks of ducts, pipes, conduits and wires' below the ground and out of sight, making modern cities appear to hum along seamlessly. 'Power, water and transport services became normalized within broader constructions of urban consumptions and culture. Increasingly, they were also delivered within public or private monopolies constructed at urban, regional or national scales as part of the wider elaboration of national welfare states.'[17] Critically, there was an underlying assumption that basic water, power, sewerage and communications services were public goods or at least quasi-public goods. In other words, they were planned, financed and managed in a way that envisaged universal coverage irrespective of the economic position of the population. And, of course, after the Great Depression of 1929, and thereafter the post-World War II era, there was certainly no shortage of poor people in these cities. Underlying this trend was a deeply held 'high-modern ideal of a unitary, orderly city, integrated by networked infrastructure.'[18]

This ideal was never fully realized in Northern cities, and was only seen to apply to the settler segments of colonial cities and towns in the developing or colonized world. In fact, a central plank of the regime of governmentality in many colonies was precisely to use infrastructure as the marker of inclusion and exclusion; the emblem of colonizer/civilized and colonized/savage. It is important to keep this in mind when one reflects on the dramatic numbers of urbanites in today's cities who have either limited or no access to basic services. Many of these cities were never intended or designed to service their populations. Graham and Marvin suggest that the Western ideal of universal service coverage has come under severe attack during the past three decades – again, at the same moment that the second wave of urbanization picked up pace. Graham explains:

> Standardized public and private infrastructure monopolies are receding as hegemonic forms of infrastructure management. We are starting to witness the uneven overlaying and retrofitting of new, high performance urban infrastructures onto the apparently immanent, universal and (usually) public monopoly network laid down between the 1930s and 1960s. In a parallel process, the diverse political and regulatory regimes that supported the 'roll-out' of power, transport, communications and water networks towards the rhetorical goal of standardized ubiquity are, in many cities and states, being 'unbundled' or even 'splintered', as a result of widespread movements towards privatization and liberalization.... What this amounts to ... is the uneven emergence of an array of what I call 'premium network spaces': new or retrofitted transport, telecommunications, power and water infrastructures that are customized precisely to the needs of the powerful users and spaces, whilst bypassing less powerful users and spaces.[19]

This radical and highly inequitable urban management agenda can be traced empirically through four interrelated processes: 'the "unbundling" of urban infrastructure provision; the erosion of comprehensive urban planning and the construction of new consumption spaces; the emergence of infrastructural consumerism; and the widespread shift towards extended and auto-mobilized cityscapes.'[20]

In the first instance, the unbundling of urban infrastructure provision takes place through privatization and/or corporatization. The latter refers to institutional models where the state retains ownership of an entity but adopts private-sector management principles and

governance structures to improve its efficiency. Typically, corporatization includes a move away from cross-subsidization of services
to a model where users pay or they are not allowed to access the
service. The country-by-country experiences of these processes are
highly unique and complex, well beyond the scope of my discussion.
The point I want to make here is that with the movement towards
the privatization or corporatization of infrastructure for services,
the potential for cross-subsidization to afford a better quality of life
for the urban poor diminishes. In fact, what happens is that user
markets get finely segmented and those who want optimal levels of
service insist that they get access to a level of quality that is com-
mensurate with what they pay. Given their political clout as a class,
those who can afford optimal levels of service tend to get what
they want. Also, in many developing countries, as explained before,
where governments are desperate to attract foreign investors, they
often subsidize and/or prioritize the infrastructure needs of TNC
investors over local populations. As a consequence, infrastructures
are embedded in ways that connect the wealthy parts of cities to the
global economy, particularly with respect to communications and
transportation, often bypassing large swathes of the city inhabited
by the poor.

The second aspect is the erosion of comprehensive urban planning
in favour of project-based infrastructure investment. If one thinks
about this for a moment, it is a completely expected consequence
of the first trend. As the private sector enters the infrastructure
market, their primary concerns will be profit maximization and the
minimization of risk. These imperatives compel them to insulate their
infrastructure projects from economic leakage by cross-subsidizing
those who cannot afford to pay for the service. Furthermore, they will
see a large population without the means to pay as a risk to achieving
their projected return on investment. As a result, their entry into the
market will often be contingent on contractual agreements with the
state that they can ring-fence their project from larger problems in
the city. The predictable consequence of this is that the urban territory is further Balkanized between those areas where infrastructure
is profitably provided and those areas without.[21] Typically, in these
cases, the state also does not have the resources or revenue streams

to extend infrastructure networks to the poor because it has lost the advantage of economies of scale.

The third aspect, the construction of infrastructural consumerism, refers to the growing tendency to tailor infrastructure provision to a highly differentiated segmentation of the population. Retailers have for some time, of course, used consumer segmentation and geodemographic targeting techniques to construct and expand brands and ensure sustained market share. In the post-Fordist era of fine-grained market segmentation, linked to ever more finely tuned product design and marketing (so that all consumers can feel like very special individuals), the same rationale has spilled over into the domain of infrastructure provision. To illustrate the power and significance of market segmentation, I reproduce a segmentation of Cape Town (my place of residence), into nine categories that coincide with income, settlement characteristics and percentage of total suburbs and households (Table 2.3). The starkest and most recognizable example of infrastructure consumerism is the dramatic rise of gated suburbs across the urban world. In these gated settlements, developers offer high-income earners an exclusive existence with access to very high quality communications infrastructure, state-of-the-art security, often with private security firms, dedicated cleaning services, and so forth. These infrastructural designs are tailor-made to the needs and aspirations of the segments of these cities that can afford to pay a premium for services, but it also means that this income becomes lost to a larger, publicly controlled investment and development strategy to address the full gamut of need across the urban territory. Infrastructural enclaves such as gated communities invariably sediment the fragmentation of urban infrastructure and space as well as reducing the capacity of the state to fulfil its public good role to ensure equitable access and patterns of development.

The fourth dimension of splintering urbanism is the rise of the polynucleated urban region and decentralization. A disturbing trend in most medium, large and mega cities across the South is to emulate the American urban form of long, stretched-out, sprawl-like developments that enable their middle classes in particular to live a consumption-driven, car-based and insular existence. In the North and some of the early urbanizing areas of the South, the trend towards car-oriented

TABLE 2.3   Geodemographic segmentation of Cape Town[22]

Cluster group	Key characteristics	% of suburbs	% of households
Silver spoons	Elite, largest consumers, getting richer	14	7
Upper middle class	Established, mature, conservative, professionals, gated	19	9
Middle suburbia	Tight budgets, mid-level jobs, bargain hunters, big spending on educating children	20	10
Community nests	Mixed, Afro-cosmo, shifting, small spaces, stylish, café culture, dense	1.5	2
Labour pool	High-density family neighbourhoods, stable jobs, secondary education, struggling	9.5	6
New bonds	New SA families, youngish, targets of the developers	13.5	13
Township living	Old places, few jobs, youth cultures, soul of the new South Africa, buzzy, vulnerable	4.5	11
Towering density	Teetering, high hopes, few options, the educated leave as soon as possible, limited reinvestment	13	22
Dire straits	Old places, overcrowded, services collapsing, high unemployment, decaying	2	3
Below the breadline	Shack settlements, desperation, insecurity	3	15

sprawl has been reinforced by the costs associated with retrofitting old infrastructure in urban cores installed in the first half of the twentieth century. This trend, in turn, has combined with engineered consumer demand for greenfield sites that can guarantee high-modern, clean-slate property developments unencumbered by the fabric of the historical built environment. In these spaces the ideal of insulated modern lifestyles is ostensibly guaranteed, a desire that feeds off the rising levels of urban fear as violence and insecurity escalate in the context of profound social inequalities. The underlying thread of these two tendencies is the mass diffusion of car cultures – the quintessential emblem of modernity in many developing countries.[23] The car culture that produces kilometres of asphalt and concrete that carries the middle-classes to their secure suburban enclaves are of course part of 'a whole system of supportive infrastructure, from highways to service stations, to drive-through fast food centres and out-of-town malls and auto-access leisure and retail complexes.'[24]

It is important to appreciate that the dramatic shift in approach to urban infrastructure, whether economic, social or public, was underpinned by a profound ideological argument that states, whether in the North or South, were the problem, not the solution. This neoliberal logic suggested that key to sustained prosperity was to create an 'enabling' or liberating environment for markets to function optimally because the only durable solution to the crises of employment and sustained economic growth was unfettered competition. This neoliberal consensus arose from neoclassical economic models and very quickly found expression in institutional theory, which informed how states had to be reorganized to become more lean, strategic and enabling, as opposed to being geared towards a mass delivery of public services. The problem for many developing countries in the 1980s was that the influential bilateral agencies dealing with development support all subscribed to this ideological outlook and tied their financial and technical support to compulsory reforms to bring market forces into play in national and especially urban management functions.[25]

Again, it is important to stress that these processes were unfolding at the precise time that agricultural activities went through the floor and large numbers of people were forced to seek a viable life and prospects in towns and cities. As a consequence, cities with highly inadequate urban infrastructure adopted an approach in which the state abdicated from investing in urban infrastructure in favour of policies that would attract private-sector actors into the infrastructure markets. Of course, as explained earlier, private-sector firms were in

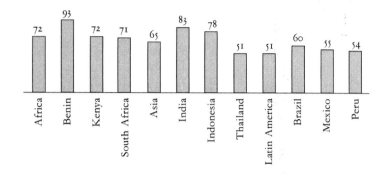

FIGURE 2.1   Scale of informal economic activity in developing countries: informal employment as % of non-agricultural employment, selected regions and countries, various years (1995–2000)[26]

the business of making a profit and would only cherry-pick low-risk and high-return projects tied to profitable segments of the economy while refusing to enter into delivery arrangements if the users could not pay market-based consumption fees. This absurd scenario played out somewhat differently in many cities where (local) politicians were so deeply embedded in economic activity that they simply could not be bothered to figure out what needed to be done to address the vast and ever growing need for urban services by many people too poor to pay. Against this backdrop, it is not surprising to learn that in most urban areas in sub-Saharan Africa informal settlements and economic activities, largely unmoored from urban infrastructure, unless clandestinely tapped into it, are the norm not the exception. The African situation may be extreme but it is certainly not isolated. Informality is increasingly the most prominent form of urban growth in very many parts of the South (see Figure 2.1).

The rise and rise of slums

Slums are a further expression of structural informality. According to the United Nations, there are four indicators that express the physical condition of slums: 'lack of water, lack of sanitation, over-crowding and non-durable housing structures. These indicators, also known as shelter deprivations, focus attention on the circumstances

TABLE 2.4 Regional distribution of the world's urban slum dwellers (2001)[27]

Region	Total urban population (1,000s)	Slum dwellers as % of region total
Sub-Saharan Africa	231,052	71.9
Asia Pacific	1,211,540	43.2
Latin America and Caribbean	399,385	31.9
Middle East and North Africa	145,624	29.5
Transition economies	259,091	9.6
Advanced economies	676,492	5.8
World	2,921,184	31.6
Developing countries	2,021,665	43.0
Least developed countries	179,239	78.2

surrounding slum life, depicting deficiencies and casting poverty as an attribute of the environment in which slum dwellers live. The fifth indicator – security of tenure – has to do with legality, which is not as easy to measure or monitor, as the status of slum dwellers often depends on de facto or de jure rights, or lack of them.'[28] Based on this definition, the UN produces a number of informative statistical overviews.

It is anticipated that all future growth of slum populations will occur exclusively in the developing world. Figure 2.2 captures the projections of slum growth up to 2020, which demonstrates clearly that the vast bulk of new slum dwellers will be in Africa and Asia. However it is important to bear in mind the substantial number of existing slum dwellers in other parts of the developing world whose living conditions are unlikely change in the near future, if current conditions remain similar into the future.

Based on these projections, senior UN–Habitat officials conclude:

> Poverty and inequality will characterize many developing-world cities, and urban growth will become virtually synonymous with slum formation in some regions. Asia is already home to more than half of the

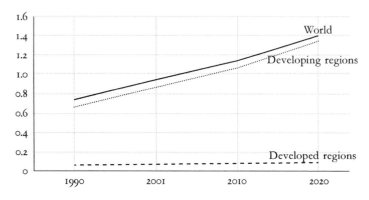

FIGURE 2.2   Slum population projections, 1990–2020 (millions)[29]

global slum population (581 million), followed by sub-Saharan Africa (199 million), which has both the highest annual urban growth rate (4.58 per cent) and the highest slum growth rate (4.53 per cent), and Latin America and the Caribbean (134 million).[30]

This is a startling acknowledgement if one considers the Habitat Agenda Declaration of 1996 made at the Habitat II global conference in Istanbul. That event emerged with a sense of confidence and optimism that the world understood what was required to achieve a turnaround in the shelter, governance and poverty crises that characterized most cities in the South. I will return to these policy agendas in the next two chapters, so will refrain from unpacking and reflecting on them here.

What is important to draw attention to in this context-setting discussion is the qualitative aspects of everyday life in slums, especially since the emerging consensus seems to be that they will become a major part of our urban future and may even be the dominant form of urbanism in much of the South, especially Africa. The first point to make is that slums are in no way homogenous or essentially the 'same' in different cities and towns and across national and regional categories. There is a real danger that the material deprivation that accompanies slum life becomes the sole lens through which these communities, households and urban actors are understood and engaged. Moreover, whilst policymakers and academics struggle to come to terms with the pervasive nature of slums, slum dwellers of course get on with the business of living, loving, exploring, working, no matter how dangerous, precarious or erratic it may be. Noble interventions by outside agencies to 'improve' the living conditions of slum dwellers or enhance their 'livelihoods' can easily be initiated at a complete disjuncture from how people hold their (precarious) lives and aspirations together, and potentially, inadvertently, undermine very delicate survival practices.

Second, slum areas are not ungoverned, even though the formal state institutions may have little administrative oversight or engagement with these communities because of the absence of household services, effective policing, health care and the like. Ethnographic and literary research is unambiguous about the multiple layers of governing that fill or rework the vacuum the state creates by its absence or obsolescence. The most obvious, and in some cases visible, presence is that of criminal gangs that use the illegibility and density of slums to anchor their production and smuggling activities. Insights into these dynamics in Kingston, Rio de Janeiro and Cape Town show a very similar symbiotic relationship between increasingly transnational criminal syndicates and local populations that provide the foot soldiers, surveillance and often physical protection for these gangs.[31] The gangs in turn invest in the social and other services of the community to prevent outright destitution but never to the extent that they actually solve anything for the long term. Within this patronage relationship there is also almost always a palpable current of fear, as these gangs use in part a regime of violence and intimation to entrench their control and sovereignty. Strikingly, alongside drug- or weapons-smuggling gangs, most slums are also sutured by a variety of religious organizations that offer respite and rationality to make sense of the drudgery of always hustling to keep destitution at bay. In addition to these two dominant forms of social structure there are also a myriad other, often more fluid and provisional, social structures that provide an entry into various networks of engagement, opportunity, pleasure, risk, exploration and mobility.[32] These social fields are composed of highly improvised (popular) cultural, ethnic, economic, trading, political and self-help groups. This social–cultural morphology suggests dense, sometimes conflictual, and always highly

TABLE 2.5   Cost of water in Accra, Ghana (2006)[33]

Water source	Cost ($/100 l.)	Users
Sachet (500 ml.)	8.01	General public, street drinking
Sachets (30-pack)	4.45	General public, household drinking
Bucket from kiosk	1.87	Households relying on shared standpipe
Community shower	1.33	Informal settlement dwellers, bathing only
Vendor	0.27	Mixed-income neighbourhood without access to piped water
Water pipe	0.05	Households with pipe connection

precarious settings within which urban development policy must intervene. It is very hard to find a full appreciation of these counter- or para-governmentalities at work in most policy models that emanate from mainstream urban development agencies. I shall explore this theme more closely in the next chapter.

Finally, from a normative, rights-based point of view, it is imperative to underscore that even though it is a highly complex and tricky affair to intervene in slums without making the situation even worse because of uni-dimensional assumptions about what is really going on, it is also clear that interventions are required. The UN–Habitat is absolutely correct to draw attention to the fact that 'Slums, and the informal economic of which they are a part, are the physical manifestation of urban poverty.'[34] Furthermore, the projected continuation of 'inequality in access to services, housing, land, education, health care and employment opportunities within cities [has] socio-economic, environmental and political repercussions, including rising violence, urban unrest, environmental degradation and underemployment.'[35] One simple illustration reinforces the point forcefully: the urban poor of Accra who reside in slums without access to piped water pay exponentially more for access compared to other urban residents in the city, as graphically illustrated in Table 2.5. It is therefore essential to use the political and policy opening in mainstream debates around the 'crisis' of unprecedented slum growth to foster a more ambitious, radical and transformative politics, as suggested in later chapters. However, this will only be possible if one can shift the underlying assumptions of mainstream policy models about the kind of politics and power relations that will indeed push forward systemic change.

What is to be done about urbanization?

The *urbanization of poverty* constitutes one of the major challenges of our times. Its underlying causes are well known – rapid and unprecedented urban growth, inequitable distribution of wealth, and the inability of the formal economy to create sufficient jobs, combined with the failure of public policy to secure people's access to basic needs.[36]

This is a profound analysis from the Head of UN–Habitat of what perpetuates the conditions outlined in this chapter; in crude terms, it is 70 per cent economics and 30 per cent state failure. This coincides very closely with the argument I have been presenting here: locating the responsibility of municipalities to deal with accelerated rates of urbanization at the same moment as the global economy undergoes a series of deep structural changes, which drives particular territorial imperatives. For example, the rise of more design-intensive and export-oriented manufacturing activity drives a demand for high-quality transport, communications and freight logistics infrastructures. Similarly, those countries in the South that can be classified as middle-income countries seek to compete with each other and Northern countries to attract ever larger slices of the rapidly growing and highly lucrative finance-related services sectors as well as tourism. In a world of fierce competition, governments see it as imperative to prioritize economic infrastructures, whether it be for export-oriented manufacturing or growing service sectors, above the social reproductive ones that especially poor households require to improve their living conditions. What these trends point to is the profundity of the policy, governance and, one could even argue, legitimacy dilemmas urban development decision-makers and activists face in the global South. My central contention is that the policy frameworks and tools promoted by mainstream development agencies such as UN–Habitat and the Cities Alliance do not help local actors to make decisions in a way that advances transformative urban change. They certainly do not empower them to deal decisively with economic inequality and structural unemployment – defined as the key underpinning of urban poverty, by the leader of UN–Habitat. As the following two chapters will demonstrate at greater length, the mainstream urban development approach operates on the following assumptions about how to respond effectively to the urbanization of poverty, which is the core story implicit in the existing and forecasted growth of slums:

- As a start, recognize the need for explicit engagement with the phenomenon of urbanization since many states, especially in sub-Saharan Africa, still operate in a default mode that believes the answer to uneven and underdevelopment is rural development.
- Once the political awareness is in place, swiftly move to an effective multi-level governmental response, which includes a national policy framework on urbanization and within a decentralized model, programmatic and financial support for municipalities to respond to the various dimensions of urbanization: appropriate land management policies, tenure security, integrated policies (as opposed to sectoral responses) to ensure affordable access to basic services, and democratic participation.
- Reform governance institutions to enable better coordination and coherence between the state, business, labour organizations and civil society organizations. Ideally, the coherence will come from a shared vision for the city or town about where it wants to position itself in the medium to long term and translate into concrete programmes that will see them, in unison, marching towards that vision.
- Finally, create a variety of partnerships between the state and business, or the state and civil society organizations, to deliver on the various needs of the urban poor and respond to the imperatives of 'sustainable' urban development.

This, admittedly crude and stylized, summary of the essence of the mainstream urban development approach can be discerned in both of the leading global campaigns of UN–Habitat – 'shelter for all' and 'good urban governance' – developed to drive urban policy reform. This policy model is deeply flawed because it is unlikely to galvanize urban actors who are interested in and committed to economic justice to find their voice and drive systemic reforms. Why? On the one hand, the UN–Habitat campaigns argue for increased investment in slum prevention, more participatory democracy, pro-poor tenure policies, and so on; and on the other hand, they support and legitimate economic development policies that focus on improving the business climate, prioritizing economic infrastructure in order to attract investment, privatizing or corporatizing certain urban services where appropriate, offering growth-enhancing tax incentives, and so on. These policy approaches are not readily compatible, and, in the absence of a clear hierarchy of public good before private gain, it is inevitable that such a policy muddle creates an ideal set of conditions for those with power and influence in the city to reproduce their interests, at the expense of the poor, with little difficulty. In my reading, the primary reason we are left with such a problematic model of urban development is the undertheorization and underemphasis of contestation-based politics that can surface and engage with power differentials in the city. It is exactly this question, then, that animates my reviews of the two primary urban development policy planks: shelter for all (reviewed in Chapter 3) and good urban governance, linked to city development strategies (reviewed in Chapter 4). The remainder of the book then proceeds to offer a different conceptual approach, which works through the useful aspects of the mainstream models but pushes it beyond their limitations.

Conclusion

The second wave of urbanization, which is largely confined to the South, could not have come at a worse time. When technological innovations offered solutions to the challenge of sanitation, health and reliable access to energy, these were assumed to be a public good, and ostensibly provided for urban populations in the North. This ideal persisted even in times of deep economic crisis and especially in post-war reconstruction times. However, as many cities and towns in the South come to be confronted with equivalent challenges, they are under tremendous pressure to think of urban infrastructure in relation to securing optimal productive platforms for mobile local and global capital, and to subject the institutional forms of service delivery to market actors, or at least market forces. This is creating a dualistic urban system: the globally connected infrastructural enclaves in the city versus the informal, almost disconnected and abandoned city, where the urban poor are subjected to inhumane living conditions.

In telling this particular story (there are many others that can be told given the great variety and complexity of urban change) I have obviously not covered a range of pertinent and increasingly pivotal issues. For example, I have said nothing about the fact that the vast majority of urbanites in the South actually live in small and medium-sized cities, contrary to the popular focus on mega (10 million plus) and meta (20 million plus) cities. It is envisaged that the current proportion of 60 per cent of urban dwellers who live in urban settlements with populations smaller that 1 million (10 per cent) and smaller than 0.5 million (51 per cent) will continue to remain into the foreseeable future. This reality represents very different conditions to the ones typically discussed in relation to 5 million plus (7 per cent) and 10 million plus (9 per cent) cities. I have also said nothing about the demographic character of cities and towns in the South; the fact that a distinctive youth bulge will shape the dominant identity and character of these places. Equally, I have ignored the growing debate on climate change and cities, and how this particular policy option is breathing new life into the urban sustainability agendas. Lastly, I have only hinted at the fact that categories of work (if work can be found) are profoundly different to what urban dwellers in the South knew or had access to just one generation ago. Given the centrality of work to questions of identity, social capital, household structures and the like, this is pivotal in understanding the nature and dynamics of urban life in the South. Given the limited length of this book, it is obviously impossible to cover all of the relevant issues. What I have decided is to structure the review and analysis to get at the nub of the dominant policy models that purport to advance an agenda of democratic inclusion, economic justice and cultural pluralism. It is now time to consider in greater detail mainstream urban development solutions.

3

Mainstream agenda 1:

shelter for all

> We reaffirm our commitment to the full and progressive realization
> of *the right to adequate housing*, as provided for in international instru-
> ments.... We commit ourselves to the goal of improving living and
> working conditions on an equitable and sustainable basis, so that
> everyone will have adequate shelter that is healthy, safe, secure,
> accessible and affordable and that includes basic services, facili-
> ties and amenities, and will enjoy freedom from discrimination in
> housing and legal security of tenure. [Moreover,] providing legal
> security of tenure and equal access to land to all people, including
> women and those living in poverty; and undertaking legislative
> and administrative reforms to give women full and equal access
> to economic resources, including the right to inheritance and to
> ownership of land and other property, credit, natural resources and
> appropriate technologies. (*Habitat Agenda*, paras 40 and 40(b))

The right to adequate housing was heavily contested at the Habitat
II Conference in Istanbul in June 1996, primarily because the United
States was vehemently opposed to it. This is one battle it lost, not
least because newcomer on the global scene, South Africa, took
a very strong position on the issue. Correctly, progressives in the
urban development field celebrated the endorsement of a rights-based
approach to housing, shelter and, by extension, land, as a momentous
victory. However, by 2004, UN–Habitat admitted that 'since the City

Summit in Istanbul, it has become all too apparent that the conditions of the world's poor have not been improved, but have continued to deteriorate.'[1] Thus, on the heels of the authoritative *The Challenge of Slums: Global Report on Human Settlements 2003*, UN–Habitat unveiled a refined agenda to drive the 'Global Campaign for Secure Shelter'. Since this document distils most clearly the organization's view on shelter, and consolidates arguments made in previous publications and related programmatic documents, I will restrict my discussion in this chapter to its contents. In reviewing the various policy pronouncements of UN–Habitat it is clear that this document is the most developed expression of the mainstream perspective on dealing with the overwhelming growth of slums and the poverty associated with it in most parts of the South.

What is particularly refreshing about the position paper (hereafter referred to as 'the Advocacy Tool') is that it allows for complexity and multiple tenure conditions as they have historically emerged in different parts of the world. It studiously seeks to avoid a simple 'one-size-fits-all' approach but at the same time is very clear and strong on what it regards as the fundamental elements of a rights-based approach to shelter. The Advocacy Tool is also clear about the scale and significance of market failure with respect to the rights of the urban poor in terms of tenure security and access to shelter. This is noteworthy given the impact of Hernando de Soto's rabid free-market tract *The Mystery of Capital*, which appeared a few years before and found great favour among many development agencies. One of the questionable aspects of the Advocacy Tool's conceptual approach is the continued promotion of the discourse of slum eradication. On the one hand it is understandable because it emerges out of Goal 7, target 11: 'the improvement of the lives of at least 100 million slum dwellers by the year 2020', but on the other hand it is also clear that slum-eradication discourses can easily become a foil for perpetuating illegal slum evictions, as we witnessed in Harare (Zimbabwe) in 2005 and 2006.

In light of this, what follows in this chapter is first a brief contextualization of the shelter-for-all campaign and its links with the broader campaigns that flow from the Millennium Development Goals (MDGs). Thereafter I explore the six core tenets of the shelter-for-all campaign, paying particular attention to the arguments and approach with regard to tenure security. The following section explores five policy areas that arise from this campaign and require more thought and deepening if the transformative potential of this campaign is to be realized.

Context of the shelter for all campaign

The Millennium Summit in September 2000 was an attempt by the United Nations to redefine its relevance and role in the global development effort. It coincided with a shift in mood in mainstream development policy ideas in the aftermath of the Asian crisis and an acknowledgement by World Bank economists such as Joseph Stiglitz that there was something fundamentally wrong with the neoliberal orthodoxy about free markets, decreasing state involvement through privatization and the disregard for the environmental and social consequences of the 'growth-is-all-you-need' model of development. In this ideological milieu the UN attempted to carve out a new development consensus that was premissed on human rights, a strong developmental role for the state and regulated economic development that was more socially inclusive and environmentally conscious, if not quite sustainable. However, in the aftermath of the long list of global development conferences since the Rio Environmental Summit in 1992, there was also a determination to be more practical, concrete and outcome-oriented in establishing a development consensus. The Millennium Development Goals were thus born and address eight areas: poverty and hunger; primary education; women's equality; child mortality; maternal health; disease; environment; and a global partnership for development. Each goal was further broken down into specific targets to be achieved by 2015, with the exception of the slum improvement target, which was set for 2020.

Target 11, in conjunction with target 10, which deals with safe drinking water and sanitation, became an important galvanizing point for UN–Habitat as it also repositioned itself – after a period of internal pressure and attack within the UN family – to become more vocal and effective. Thus, UN–Habitat restructured itself to do four primary tasks with regard to slum eradication: monitoring secure tenure and slum upgrading; analysis of political, social and economic factors that impact on tenure and informal settlements;

campaigning through rights-based advocacy around the solutions available to achieve the target; and promoting operational readiness in member states through policy reform and capacity-building that can support 'instruments for the improvements in tenure security, shelter, services, and employment in slum areas.'[2]

In light of this policy-institutional approach, the Global Campaign for Secure Tenure (GCST) became the central plank to advance the commitments member states made in the Habitat Agenda to providing Adequate Shelter for All. The GCST, at the highest design level, focused on preventative and adaptive strategies. The former focuses on a perspective and response that moves away from trying to stop migration from rural to urban areas, but rather concentrates on how such patterns can be slowed down and managed more effectively to realize a more dispersed pattern of urban settlements, more amenable to economic and social management. Adaptive strategies are defined on the basis that developing countries need to come to terms with the enduring reality of large-scale informal settlements. Once acceptance occurs, a substantial policy scaffolding needs to be developed and instituted. The adaptive focus provides guidance on what these policies are and how best to institutionalize them in various contexts. The absolute starting point of adaptation is an unambiguous move to ensure security of tenure. Thereafter, a vast array of policy considerations come into play.

> In practical terms, adaptive strategies are cost-effective programmes and projects aimed at providing, in a sustainable manner: Decent housing or house improvement schemes, including micro-credit for low cost housing; a range of affordable tenure options which give tenure security to the poor; Water and sanitation; Disaster preparedness and prevention; Community-led safer cities initiatives; Solid waste management services; Transport infrastructure and services; Attracting investment through appropriate regulatory framework [*sic*] and increased productivity; Environmentally sound urban policies; Promoting inclusion, gender awareness and participatory decision making; and Building local capacities through decentralization, legislative and institutional change and strengthening local governments.[3]

However, this rather ambitious longer-term agenda is pursued through a more methodical focus on what the Campaign toolkit calls 'key messages':

- Protecting and promoting housing rights for all to ensure enjoyment of full urban citizenship for the urban poor.
- Secure tenure is essential for city stability, human dignity and urban development.
- Gender equity: promoting the role of women in development and the removal of all discrimination.
- Partnership: city governments working with people's organizations can promote sustainable urban development.
- There should be an alternative to forced evictions which violate human rights, in the form of negotiated resettlement if necessary.
- Provision of transparent and accessible information on urban land markets can reduce corruption and speculation.
- Provision of affordable well-located land for human settlement is essential for the future of the city.[4]

I explore each of these themes in closer detail in the next section, although the main emphases fall on tenure security, civil society participation and the regulation of land markets, before I conclude with reflections on the silences in the campaign.

Tenets of the global campaign for secure tenure

As I signalled in the introduction to the chapter, this policy framework set out by UN–Habitat is astute and impressive given the range of interests and issues that it needs to balance. In particular, given my broader argument in the book for deepening a rights-based approach to urban transformation, I find the centrality of a rights discourse useful and important. The GCST advocacy framework explicitly identifies it as a major problem and weakness in the overall shelter effort that the right to housing is largely ignored and frequently violated. In response, the GCST seeks to draw attention to the legal obligations on states to take it seriously, and has enrolled the Office of the United Nations High Commissioner for Human Rights, who in turn has appointed a Special Rapporteur on adequate housing. Interestingly, in 2007 the Special Rapporteur carried out a review of South Africa's housing policies and programmes. In one recommendation he points out the imperative for South Africa: 'To consider intervention in the market to regulate the current high and unaffordable prices, and to check against land and property speculation.'⁵ This is fascinating because it is, of course, the dominance of property rights, particularly private property rights, which are enshrined in the constitution, that play a big part in the inability of South Africa to give effect to the progressive realization of housing rights. Unfortunately, the tension between private property rights and housing rights are left hanging in the GCST, which weakens the transformative potential of the document. This is a curious oversight since the document itself recognizes the role of unregulated, speculative land markets in perpetuating slums.

Tenure security

The guts of the GCST, and its strongest conceptual part, is the discussion on tenure security. The overarching argument of the document is that the most important reform to achieve in the push towards the broader goal of shelter for all, as envisioned in the Habitat Agenda, is to address the large-scale problem of tenure insecurity. From this vantage point, the campaign prioritizes tenure security as opposed to promoting particular kinds of tenure. In fact, the GCST advocacy tool usefully spells out the spectrum of tenure relations that can be found; what needs to be done at the macro level to improve the overall context of tenure security; and then how to put in place a system to bring greater certainty and clarity to what will invariably be a very complex and fluid tenure scenario. And, because of the wide spectrum of tenure arrangements (see Box 3.1 below) that it regards as prevalent and in complex relation to each other, the policy framework points to the potential dangers associated with rapid regularization of land ownership to achieve individual freehold title because of potential unintended consequences such as market eviction through downward raiding.⁶ The perspective of the GCST comes through particularly clearly in the following argument:

> Land tenure and property rights are more complicated than the con-
> ventional categories of legal/illegal, or formal/informal suggest. Most
> urban areas contain a range of semi-legal categories and maybe even
> more than one legal system, as in countries where statutory, customary
> and religious tenure co-exist. In this sense, it is preferable to consider

tenure and property rights as a continuum with different shades of grey as well as black and white categories. Land tenure issues reflect cultural, historical and political influences; therefore policy should recognize and reflect local circumstances.[7]

This perspective makes sense once one appreciates the range within the continuum of tenure arrangements, each with unique advantages and limitations for the urban poor, that can generally be found in urban areas in the South.

In light of this diversity, what is more important to UN–Habitat is 'residential tenure' as opposed to access to land-based freehold title, the preferred solution of Hernando de Soto.[8] The residential tenure bias is in response to the reality of informal settlements as a substantial, if not dominant, component of the urban fabric. The core issue for the GCST is the imperative to establish formal legal recognition of diverse tenure arrangements that proliferate and coexist in informal areas, because they observe that even in cases where there may be de facto administrative recognition through 'the provision of municipal and urban services, and the associated collection of revenue', insecurity in the face of exploitative discretionary authority can remain high.[9] In other words, tenure is enforceable but not justiciable, which, for UN–Habitat, disqualifies it from being considered secure tenure. This is a very significant position to take because in increasingly large portions of the developing world a situation is arising where some basic services are extended to informal areas but the underlying tenure issues are not addressed, making such investments accrue to intermediaries that control these areas beyond the regulatory purview of the state and on very exploitative terms for the urban poor.[10] Also, when market opportunities come knocking through downward raiding, there is no protection for these communities, and households will simply be washed away to another, probably more remote, insecure location.

I now want to return to the argument made by de Soto that bestowing freehold title is the most effective way to reconnect slums and informal settlements back into the mainstream fabric of the city. This is an important debate to review because most governments and private-sector interests that join up with governance partnerships or city strategy forums are likely to be seduced by the simplicity

BOX 3.1   Tenure systems and their characteristics[11]

Freehold

Provides ownership in perpetuity.

Advantages: high degree of security; freedom to dispose, or use as collateral for loans; maximizes commercial value, enabling people to realize substantial increases in asset values.

Disadvantages: costs of access generally high; collateral value may not be relevant if incomes are low or financial institutions are weak; property values can go down as well as up and may trap the unwary in properties worth less than they paid for them.

Delayed freehold

Conditional ownership: title is granted on the completion of payments or when developments have been completed.

Advantages: same high degree of security as freehold, providing payments are made as required or developments completed; freedom to dispose, or use as collateral for loans; maximizes commercial value, enabling people to realize substantial increases in asset values.

Disadvantages: failure to maintain payments or undertake developments may result in eviction and loss of funds invested; collateral value may not be relevant if incomes are low; property values can go down as well as up and may trap the unwary in properties worth less than they paid for them; expectations of increased values can divert investments from more productive sectors of the economy.

Registered leasehold

Ownership for a specified period: from a few months to 999 years.

Advantages: as secure as freehold, but only for the period specified in the lease.

Disadvantages: requires legal framework; costs of access generally high.

Public rental

Rental occupation of publicly owned land or house.

Advantages: provides a high degree of security provided terms and conditions of occupation are met.

Disadvantages: limited supply may restrict access; often badly located for access to livelihoods; terms often restrictive; deterioration if maintenance costs not met.

Private rental

Rental of privately owned land or property.

Advantages: good security; maintains social cohesion.

Disadvantages: open to abuse by disreputable owners; deterioration if maintenance costs not met.

Shared equity

Combination of delayed freehold and rental, in which residents purchase a stake in their property (often 50 per cent) and pay rent on the remainder to the other stakeholder.

Advantages: combines the security and potential increase in asset value of delayed freehold and the flexibility of rental; residents can increase their stake over time, ultimately leading to full ownership.

Disadvantages: needs legal framework and efficient management.

Co-operative tenure

Ownership is vested in the co-operative or group of which residents are co-owners.

Advantages: good security if protected by legally enforceable contract; provides tenants with flexibility of movement.

Disadvantages: requires a legal framework; restrictions may reduce incentives to invest; requires double registration first of land and of association.

Customary ownership

Ownership is vested in the tribe, group community or family. Land is allocated by customary authorities such as chiefs.

Advantages: widely accepted; simple to administer; maintains social cohesion.

Disadvantages: may lose its legal status in urban areas; vulnerable to abuse under pressure of urbanization; poor customary leadership may weaken its legitimacy.

Religious tenure systems (e.g. Islamic)

There are four main categories of land tenure within Islamic societies. *Waqf* is religious trust land and is potentially very significant in addressing landlessness, whilst *mulk*, or individual full ownership, is also protected in law; *miri*, or state owned/controlled land which carries *tassruf* or usufruct rights, is increasingly common, whilst *musha/mushtarak*, is collective/tribal ownership.

Advantages: facilitates family/group tenures and accessible and affordable land management procedures.

Disadvantages: because they are outside the commercial land market, *waqf* lands are often inefficiently managed. Inheritance disputes can cause land conflicts.

Non-formal tenure systems

These include a wide range of categories with varying degrees of legality or illegality. They include regularized and unregularized squatting, unauthorized subdivisions on legally owned land and various forms of unofficial rental arrangements. In some cases, several forms of tenure may coexist on the same plot, with each party entitled to certain rights.

Advantages: some of these non-formal categories, such as squatting, started as a response to the inability of public allocation systems or formal commercial markets to provide for the needs of the poor and operated on a socially determined basis.

Disadvantages: as demand has intensified, even these informal tenure categories have become commercialized, so that access by lower income groups is increasingly constrained.

of the freehold tenure route, which is but one in the continuum of practices prevalent in most urban areas. In his book *The Mystery of Capital*, de Soto seeks to do nothing less than solve the problem of global poverty. He provides a compelling argument which centres on the idea that the solution is already present in all cities, towns and countries, awaiting enlightened and bold decision-makers to grasp it. The solution is to transform widespread informal (or 'extra-legal' in his parlance) tenure and economic conditions into formal or legally recognized assets that individuals can use as a resource to access capital, which in turn can propel their entrepreneurial initiatives and further investments in their assets. And since the vast majority of urban dwellers live in unregistered and informal arrangements, all that is required is to transform such arrangements into formal, recognized conditions – through freehold title deeds and business permits – and the latent power and energy of the poor will be unleashed, solving the problem of poverty. This model rests on three core arguments: (i) people will only invest in their housing and business if they feel secure of their tenure status; (ii) access to credit can only be provided if there is a systematic legalization of informal settlements and business, which assumes a massive undertaking to bring all land and property into a cadastral system; and (iii) the best practical means to achieve this is to provide universal title owner-ship through individual freehold title that can result in a coherent titles system that is linked to enforceable rights.[12] Apart from Peru and many other Latin American countries where large-scale titling programmes have been and are being pursued, the Tanzanian govern-ment also commissioned de Soto and his team to run this model for Tanzania.[13] So, there should be no illusions about the impact and discourse-shaping effects of this work.

Since the publication of de Soto's *The Mystery of Capital*, a number of critical reviews of the book and, especially, the implementation of his ideas has followed. In essence these concur that none of the three pillars of the policy model holds water. For example, reviews of a large-scale titling programme in Peru, which involved the issuing of 1.4 million titles between 1996 and 2004, did not necessarily lead to access to credit. Apparently, for most lending agencies, a regular job was more important.[14] Specifically, only 1.6 per cent of titlehold-ers had obtained loans using the property as collateral by the time 76 per cent of these titles had been issued in Peru.[15] This empirical trend is a damning indictment of the essence of de Soto's model. Furthermore, empirical trends in Latin America also reveal that large numbers of people access informal credit even when there is no effective perception of tenure security. This undercuts the notion that freehold title is a precondition for access to credit.

At a deeper, legally conceptual level, Edesio Fernandez points out that what remains undeveloped or defined in de Soto's work is the sociology and political economy of legal systems: in other words, the assumption that there is 'a universal, a-historical "natural" legal definition' of property rights is simply a fiction. Historical evidence is clear, according to Fernandez, that the state treats 'different forms of property rights (financial, industrial, intellectual, etc.) and the social relations around them' differently in order to 'accommodate varying degrees of state intervention in the domain of economic property relations'.[16] As a consequence of this ahistorical perspective on legal systems and the political-cultural norms that underpin and surround them, de Soto also misses 'dialectically contradictory relationships between legality and illegality'. However, the most important and damning critique of an uncritical, ahistorical drive to conduct blanket titling to solve (urban) poverty is that it fails to appreciate the dangers of freehold title in terms of the overall urban system. Fernandez argues cogently:

> [E]xisting research has shown that while the recognition of individual freehold titles can promote individual security of legal tenure it does not necessarily entail sociospatial integration. Unless titling is undertaken within the context of a broader set of public policies that address urban, politico-institutional and socioeconomic conditions, legalization programs may actually aggravate the processes of exclusion and segregation. As a result, the original beneficiaries of the programs might not be able to remain on the legalized land, although that should be the ultimate objective of regularization programs, especially on public land.[17]

On this note, I will return to my review of the GCST advocacy tool publication. It provides a clear set of arguments around the limitations and problems associated with freehold title,[18] which echo the points levelled against de Soto. In light of this caution about freehold title, the GCST promotes a focus on rental lease and group-based forms of tenure as areas of policy thinking that require more work and, especially, improved institutional functioning where it is in fact being addressed. In fact, what emerges in the document is that the rental sector particularly is seen as key:

> [F]or low-income families, rental – which is the most used form of tenure – is seldom formal or regulated in many countries. Agreements are arrived at informally, with little or no recourse to legal advice, and the agreements are enforced in a non-legal manner. Indeed, a major part of the campaign will have to address the urban-poor segment of the rental sector, and the tension that exists between secure tenure for tenants and sub-tenants, and the property rights of the owners. Both in percentage and in policy terms, addressing the informal rental sector will be one of the most significant challenges for the campaign, and on which will have the most impact for the urban poor.[19]

However, working in the rental and group-based systems implies a high level of capability within state and support institutions, which is not a trivial matter given the low levels of effective decentralization and financial devolution that remain a dominant factor in many developing countries. In fairness, the GCST recognizes the necessity of not only institutional capability but also institutional thickness: 'Partnerships, a user-friendly justice system, [clearly a big ask], and the role of well-informed NGOs is critical in the creation of good lessor–lessee relationships.' Furthermore, the 'exclusion that women face in the titling process applies with regard to leases, and requires specific measures, such as joint registration and joint recording in the name of both spouses.'[20] What is perhaps less clear is how such capacity will be developed and what happens in the interim whilst local states get empowered and capacity is developed. Furthermore, the document fails to explain its optimism about the likely private sector involvement in providing loan finance to group-based tenure bodies.[21]

A core message of the GCST is that 'all forms of secure tenure can only be effective when they operate within an enabling legal framework, and they are supported by good governance and an administrative capacity.'[22] The question this immediately raises is, to what extent are these preconditions likely to exist? Moreover, what are the factors that militate against their existence? For example, if informalized and backstreet deal-making is the norm, how does one really engage and root out patronage-based politics? In most developing countries with relatively young or fragile democracies, political parties are embedded in the broader context of limited economic opportunities and a desperate need for access to scarce public resources. In these contexts, clientalist and patronage politics are a way of life.[23] Can weak local states be 'fixed' in a short period of time? In any case, are there any firm indicators or evidence that national political-cultural factors that undermine substantive and funded decentralization of functions are likely to change in the immediate future given trend patterns over the past decade? It is important to contextualize these lines of questioning by reference to the aftermath of devastating structural adjustment policies that have eroded national power, authority and capability. None of these central governance questions is satisfactorily addressed or even flagged in the campaign materials. Of course, there is constant reference to the linked campaign on good urban governance, but, as I show in the next chapter, these kinds of issues are not addressed in that domain of work either.

Furthermore, market pressures and trends are underestimated in the document. One reason why effective regulation of land and property markets is difficult is that developing countries are typically highly dependent on a relatively small tax-paying class that sustains the coffers of the state, and often also the individual interests of senior politicians in the ruling party and the state. Considering the impact of the globalization of property markets and, increasingly, real-estate and developer companies, it is apparent that the regulatory power of states with regard to developers and investors is limited. And, as the GCST recognizes, without strong regulatory intervention in land markets through appropriate tenure systems and land-use instruments, advancing the approach advocated for by the GCST will be very difficult. In this context, it is a serious omission that there is not a more explicit and detailed argument about specific regulations and regulating systems to structure and steer land-use patterns more effectively. Practically, I have in mind the typology proposed by Robert Riddell, which includes, inter alia: eminent domain, negoti-ated purpose, land banking, central directive, a wide array of zoning categories, growth boundary, transferable development rights, waivers, purchased development right, user levies, development bonuses.[24] It seems that an emphasis on particular kinds of tenure that are optimal for the urban poor cannot be divorced from a larger framework of urban management instruments that needs to be in place to impact decisively and effectively on urban land markets.

This gap in the approach to tenure security as a pathway to adequate shelter throws up the question, what are the elements of the bigger picture? Clearly, the first aspect is access to basic services within a framework that guarantees access for those who are too poor to pay. Also, tenure regularization must unfold in tandem with a 'locality-within-a-region' approach to the extension of basic services. In other words, infrastructure investments and maintenance systems for a particular informal settlement must be designed and planned with explicit reference to a larger urban regional approach – in part because the way services are extended and maintained offers crucial opportunities to deal with unemployment and informal service providers who can be enrolled into more regularized and context-sensitive models of delivery. In another sense, a regional approach is crucial because the infrastructural response must be consistent with regional-level objectives to achieve a more environmentally sustainable urban form and system – that is, a system that progressively reduces unsustainable patterns of consumption and production and facilitates more equitable spatial patterns and relations. I will return to this issue in the next section because it deserves more attention in urban development debates.

Last, in terms of the bigger picture agenda that should frame strategic approaches to tenure, is the question of the quality of the built environment that characterizes informal settlements, but also strategic arteries in the city that connect slums to each other and the larger urban system. When I speak of quality of the built environment I am referring to the architectural, urban design and planning criteria that inform slum-upgrading programmes. The tendency is to focus on individual households, or a small cluster of overpopulated slum clusters, but very seldom is there an explicit recognition of the centrality of design-based criteria (beyond the functional issues of cheapest material per monetary unit) to the calculus about how to improve living conditions in a slum. Brazil, Chile and Colombia have important examples of how to bring high-quality public spaces that promote security, especially the safety of women and children, and fluid movement corridors and pathways into informal areas to create a profoundly different sense of place, even if the dominant mode of shelter construction is makeshift and a hotchpotch of solid and temporary materials.[25] The important benefit of a spatial approach that is also design-rich is that it affords innovative opportunities to create democratic deliberation processes among local residents, and between them and the state, about what physical expression can be given to the identities and aspirations of a particular community. This particular issue is reinforced in Chapter 6 where I explore different aesthetic and phenomenological registers to think about and through slums. On the note of participation, I now want to turn to the UN–Habitat embracing of slum dwellers' organizations as a partner in achieving its long-term vision of shelter for all.

Secure tenure, slum upgrading and participation

The GCST is peppered with references to the importance of women's participation in improving the tenure situation of slum dwellers. There is also a fascinating discussion on the growth of vulnerable children in the context of the AIDS pandemic as a particular category of vulnerable people in informal settlements. This is a commendable conceptual and policy focus throughout the whole family of inter-related shelter and governance policy streams of both UN–Habitat and the other urban development agencies gathered together in the Cities Alliance. I have one quibble though. Throughout the document, the participation of women is equated with gender equality. There is, of course, an obvious truth to this given that in most developing countries, women remain primarily excluded from and marginalized in decision-making processes; a highly detrimental situation because the literature is fairly conclusive that development resources controlled by women tend to have better developmental outcomes, especially for children. However, it is also well established that women are not automatically in favour of gender equality and can for various cultural and social reasons be as vociferous as men in reinforcing gender stereotypes and deferring decision-making to men. In light of this it is necessary for the GCST to refine its thinking on gender equality and what is required concretely to shift both men's and women's attitudes and behaviours with regard to gender roles and a reconfiguration of power relations.

I now want to turn to the UN Millennium Task Force Report on Improving the Lives of Slums Dwellers, titled *A Home in the City* (hereafter also referred to as the 'task force report'). This report sets out compellingly what one can describe as the emerging consensus on how best to understand and transform slums in the global effort to achieve target 11 of the MDGs.[26] I want to home in on the report's robust perspective on the pivotal role of civil society organizations in addressing the challenge of slums, and, within this, particularly the position and methodology of federations of slums dwellers. This is of relevance because there is clearly cross-fertilization between what the core argument of the task force report is and the one promoted in the GCST.[27] The policy perspective adopted, and advocated, in the task force report constitutes an important shift in mainstream thinking about effective interventions to address urban slums.

A Home in the City followed closely on the heels of the important UN–Habitat Global Report on Human Settlements of 2003, *The Challenge of Slums.* In this report the paradigm-shift away from a narrow slum clearance/sanitation approach to one of gradual systematic improvement in partnership with slum dwellers was unambiguously consolidated. Furthermore, *The Challenge of Slums* also went to considerable lengths to demonstrate the structural underpinnings of urban inequality that frame the formation and growth of slums in the world; again, a critical political economy perspective that further opened the door for progressive civil society interests to advance arguments about the importance of a politicized rights-based discourse in dealing with understanding and improving slum areas. As I suggested at the outset, these recent shifts in mainstream policy discourses are undoubtedly important achievements in promoting a more transformative approach to urban development politics and praxis.

Given the salience of a savings-based mobilization methodology of organizing slum dwellers, it is fitting to reflect more critically on this 'achievement.' It seems to me that that there was a 'thinning' of social life and sociality in slum areas in the imaginary about social citizenship that was being invoked by the emerging consensus. I am therefore ambivalent about the elevation of a particular social mobilization model of various homeless people's federations across the world as necessarily the most effective way of building onto capacities within poor communities. My ambivalence stems from the fact that I agree with much of the analysis in the UN Millennium Task Force's report about the methodology and effectiveness of these organizations (see chapter 2 in the report), and further appreciate the strategic significance of having such a bottom-up democratic perspective ensconced in global discourses about urban development; yet, at the same time, I am concerned about the reification of a particular social mobilization model with respect to expressing social citizenship in the context of urban slums[28] (in Chapter 6, I underscore the importance of these movements).

There are indeed outstanding features in the methodology that member federations of Shack/Slum Dwellers International have forged organically over time, and mostly through tough struggles, but it remains a model that emerged in very particular cultural-historical circumstances. When a grassroots methodology is elevated to a generic mode of social intervention, it potentially runs into problems. For example, a review of the South African Homeless People's Federation revealed that elements of the savings-based model do not work in all contexts. Significantly, the model tends to 'impose' a moral regime on the participants in the movements that holds the potential of being authoritarian, especially when internal democratic processes and cultures are still nascent. As a result, the highly disciplined and ritualistic methodology of these organizations does draw strong lines of inclusion and exclusion inside the communities where they operate, even though they supposedly operate on non-sectarian principles. This is not to detract from the excellent work the various federations do but merely to flag that putting forward their model as the approach for civil society participation in slum improvement and prevention is not without dangers. The increasingly influential task force report does not go far enough to unpack some of these issues.

What's more, and related, the task force report and the GCST tend to treat the four stakeholder groups – organizations of the poor, the private sector, government and NGOs – in slum improvement and prevention as too homogenous. On the civil society side this tendency leads to a too-narrow focus on a particular model of poor people's organization. On the private sector side the focus is simply on leveraging investment and not broader issues such as the roles that can arise from different categories of business. Private-sector behaviour in general in shaping market sentiments about appropriate and optimal levels of redistribution in a society is as important as the material contribution of the private sector through financing of urban infrastructure. As a result there is not enough emphasis in either report on the broader environment-shaping role of the private sector that shapes discursive boundaries about how the slums question is defined in societal terms and, most importantly, what everyone in the city can do to intervene. This goes to the question of culpability in the growth and persistence of slums and associated living conditions in cities where the middle class live very different lives, and can potentially contribute to solving the issues through myriad contributions that address social cohesion, solidarity and bridging social capital.

Linked to the previous blind spot, slum dwellers are painted in homogenous terms, which stem from the social mobilization model and generality of the recommendations proposed in the report. Pragmatically, it is understandable that slum dwellers are depicted in one-dimensional terms, but of concern are the consequences for policymakers who come to these issues for the first time. In other words, if such decision-makers encounter real communities in all their rich and contradictory diversity, they may regard the general approach of the report as too idealistic or simply unviable. In fairness, the task force report does at certain points draw attention to how identity markers of difference can 'affect the severity with which problems are experienced', but this is not teased out strongly enough. This leads to another concern.

The task force report does not pay attention to the benefits, limited and perverse as they may be, that slum situations offer *some* of the poor who live there. Any slum improvement intervention must be sober about why it may be beneficial for some people to want to continue their livelihoods in a context of an informal settlement and not formal housing or a more formalized environment. As slums exist currently, they are teeming with life, social networks and economic linkages. It is often impossible to re-create these livelihood options and possibilities outside of highly fluid and malleable physical conditions that are best offered by informal areas. It is important to shed light on these aspects of slum life, without romanticizing them, because policymakers are often baffled by the resistance that come from some slum dwellers to upgrading proposals. Furthermore, upgrading initiatives must, of course, work with an intimate understanding of the existing livelihood strategies of those affected, as the vast literature on livelihoods and asset-based poverty reminds us. This was missed in South Africa where the government is confronted by the dilemma that people who have been awarded a 'free' house with basic services by the government sell it way below the value at the moment of transfer, only to return to an informal settlement, because they need some financial liquidity to carry out trading that can only be done in an informal setting as the land-use and property regulations are too restrictive in formal townships.

The point of this section has simply been to problematize current mainstream thinking, which has moved considerably from where it was a decade ago on questions of slum resident participation in settlement policies, in order to contribute to what I think is a valuable and potentially empowering framework for the future of urban development processes. In Chapters 4 and 5 it will become clearer how one can think more broadly and multidimensionally about civil society dynamics and participation in urban development discourses and processes.

Infrastructure and environmental dimensions

In this last section I want to dwell on the infrastructural implications of the approach to urban sustainability promoted in the GCST: 'A sustainable policy for shelter and slum upgrading also entails the promotion of linkages between service delivery, employment and income generation.'[29] This ambition is consistent with the argument made in the larger, overarching *State of Human Settlements 2003* report: 'Slum policies should seek to support the livelihoods of the urban poor, by enabling urban informal sector activities to flourish, linking low-income housing development to income generation, and ensuring easy access to jobs though pro-poor transport and low-income settlement locations policies.'[30] In this, arguably pro-poor, perspective, a vital area of major reform is missed. Yes, of course it is essential to ensure that infrastructure provision is conducted in the most labour-intensive manner and linked to procurement provisions that allows local people in the slum to be incorporated into the construction and maintenance of the infrastructure. This bias goes almost without saying, but what is arguably more important is to redefine the nature of urban areas by systematically transforming the nature and ecological impacts of urban consumption and production activities.

Practically, what this means is a much more ambitious macro-framework for urban infrastructure, which could then circumscribe particular strategies for informal areas. Mark Swilling argues that from a city-wide systems level, down to the design of neighbourhoods and households, a number of transitions need to be pursued in order to make cities simultaneously more environmentally sustainable, socially inclusive and economically resilient.[31] These transitions are:

- To renewable energy alternatives and greater energy efficiency, as renewable infrastructures require long lead times to come on stream. Significantly, from an employment perspective, campaigns to retrofit and build differently can have a substantial knock-on effect in terms of stimulating new niche market products and services; and there is no reason why these growth areas cannot be regulated to ensure absorption of unemployed people in slum areas.

- To a zero-waste position for the city or town because all waste outputs are turned into productive inputs for other economic processes. International precedents and experience make this a low-threshold reform to pursue with vigour. In fact, in most developing countries waste-recycling activities characterized by bad working conditions are widespread. However, what is missing is a broader municipal policy that builds onto and augments what urban informal recyclers have been doing all along.

- To sustainable transport systems, with a particular emphasis on public transport. Again, good practice in cities like Curitiba, Bogotá and Porto Alegre makes this a very viable area of major reform. Given the centrality of transport to a wide range of social and economic processes, this is arguably the easiest entry point to begin to reposition incrementally the infrastructure approach of a city or town. The fast-growing problem of congestion is also a good incentive to get middle-class buy-in for dramatic reform in this area.

- To the mandatory use of sustainable construction materials and building methods. Even in countries where local government is still nascent, most municipalities have the power to prescribe, in combination with national guidelines, specifications for the use of construction materials and levels of insulation that dramatically increase the energy efficiency of dwellings.

- To sustainable water use and reuse of treated sewage. Swilling points out that grey 'water re-use systems are viable at household and neighbourhood levels, and neighbourhood-level sewage treatment systems are also viable, with the treated effluent feeding into nurseries, orchards or back into houses to flush toilets. The system can be coupled to better management of the commons such as wetlands, recreational spaces, etc.'[32] There are also numerous policies to use public-works type programmes to involve large numbers of unemployed people to address leaks. Again, it is relatively easy to draw linkages between more sustainable practices and the informalized or self-organized work categories that make sense in slum contexts.

• To local and sustainable food. This is probably one of the most important and potentially rich areas of intervention. Given the environmental health conditions in many slums, the importance of good nutrition cannot be overstated. An intervention that can make a massive difference to food security and profitable urban agriculture with significant labour-absorbing potential would be neighbourhood-level markets where small-scale growers, who represent a vital counterpoint to irrigation-based food production, can display and sell their produce. Apart from the economic and health benefits, this can also greatly contribute to urban design and quality of place, issues which need more attention, as suggested earlier.

• To a city-wide commitment to reinforce and support equity and fair trade at all levels if possible. This is, of course, an area of focus that is almost reaching maturity in Northern contexts, but it seems to me that there is little preventing (particularly) middle-income countries making it fashionable for their middle classes to consume ethically and organically, where feasible.

This is obviously not a comprehensive list but it indicates that an overly narrow focus on extending basic services to the poor, without thinking about the broader environmental sustainability and job creation potential, is simply not wise at this stage. Of course, given the dominant ideologies that continue to underpin infrastructure discourses, as mentioned in Chapter 2, along with rapidly growing need and limited resources, these kinds of transition will not be that easy to make. However, nor will the tenure reforms discussed earlier, nor the desire for participation and power on the part of the urban poor to shape urban development futures.

All of these redefinitions of urban management imply dramatic changes in the orientation and capabilities of sub-national governments; they also imply a space for deep political contestation, negotiation, deliberation, agreement and more contestation because it is impossible to reorient public priorities and budgets fundamentally without a modicum of political agreement and determination. And, by definition, this has to be political engagement within sub-national states but also between government representatives and representatives from civil society organizations, business and universities. However, in reading across the various UN–Habitat policy prescriptions, one is struck by the confidence that enough participation and stakeholder engagement will produce the necessary consensus and buy-in to drive urban reform. These assumptions find their starkest expression in the Global Campaign for Urban Governance, to which I turn in the next chapter. My aim is to demonstrate that without a fully developed understanding of 'the political' – inherently conflictual power relations – in the city, the prospects of moving good policies into institutionalized practices are rather slim.

4

Mainstream agenda II:

good governance

Sustainable human settlements are those that, inter alia, generate a sense of citizenship and identity, cooperation and dialogue for the common good, and a spirit of voluntarism and civic engagement, where all people are encouraged and have an equal opportunity to participate in decision making and development. (*Habitat Agenda*, para. 32)

The increasingly central focus on the role of organizations representing slum dwellers, such as Shack/Slum Dwellers International (SDI), in the discourse of UN–Habitat and the UN Millennium Project, as discussed in the previous chapter, illustrates the rise of participatory development discourses in policy discussions on dealing with urbanization and particularly the growth of slums. In this chapter I want to explore the mainstream policy approach to urban governance as exemplified in the policy frameworks of UN–Habitat, and the increasingly influential Cities Alliance. Specifically, it requires a review of the Good Urban Governance campaign of UN–Habitat, which has been in circulation since 1999, and the Cities Development Strategy thrust of Cities Alliance. My core argument is that at a normative level the UN has made crucial advances to underwrite and extend the debate on the right to housing and, more broadly, the right to city, themes first broached at Istanbul II in 1996. However, in my reading, the underlying assumptions of both policy thrusts about local participatory democracy are deeply flawed and require closer scrutiny in order to arrive at a more robust conception of democratic governance that is conducive to greater intra-urban equity and inclusivity.

Origins and context

After a flurry of UN-sponsored international development conferences in the first half of the 1990s, it was the turn of the urban agenda to be showcased in 1996. An impressive global gathering was assembled in Istanbul – that magnificent enigma of a city that defies any form of conceptual capture – to deliberate on how best to understand and respond to the challenges of worldwide urbanization. In policy terms this gathering represented a high-water mark for sustainable and human development protagonists in the UN system who were trying to push back against the devastating effects of the narrow neoliberal economic approach that came to overshadow development policy and mainstream support during the 1980s and early 1990s. Given that cities were regarded as the centrepiece of the economic growth/productivity agendas of the World Bank, it was seen as a crucial frontier to consolidating a more holistic, democratic and integrated approach to development. This is strongly evident in the Habitat Agenda Declaration that was adopted at the end of the UN–Habitat Summit, as evidenced in the following excerpt:

> During the course of history, urbanization has been associated with economic and social progress, the promotion of literacy and education, the improvement of the general state of health, greater access to social services, and cultural, political and religious participation. Democratization has enhanced such access and meaningful participation and involvement for civil society actors, for public–private partnerships, and for decentralized, participatory planning and management, which are important features of a successful urban future. Cities and towns have been engines of growth and incubators of civilization and have facilitated the evolution of knowledge, culture and tradition, as well as of industry and commerce. Urban settlements, properly planned and managed, hold the promise for human development and the protection of the world's natural resources through their ability to support large numbers of people while limiting their impact on the natural environment.

It is important to bear in mind that by the mid-1990s, the expansion of democratic systems in the developing world was still recent. Many postcolonial experiments had run aground through authoritarianism combined with asymmetrical insertion into global markets, which saw the dramatic decline in value of primary commodities from the late 1960s. It was only towards the end of the 1970s and in the early 1980s that democratic experiments across the world started to take a foothold again, manifested in an outbreak of multiparty democratic systems during the 1980s and 1990s. This trend was further bolstered by the fall of the Berlin Wall and the symbolic disintegration of the edifice of actually existing socialism as it was practised in the Soviet Union and its surrogate states. Importantly, neoliberal economic thought also achieved its apogee during this period, a further impetus to dilute the power of the state, which happened to be by and large undemocratic and authoritarian. There was unfortunately a neat convergence between market fundamentalism associated with neoliberal economic thought and the push for multiparty democracy across the world; and in existing democracies like India or Argentina, neoliberalism flourished under the drive for state withdrawal from services delivery to counteract the perceived inefficiency and corruption of these machineries.

The point about this recollection is that by the beginning of the 1990s, the discourse of multiparty democracy was hegemonic and virtually total. However, in most developing countries this simply meant a reinforcement of state power in national government, especially the executive. Local democracy was typically underdeveloped, in large part because national departments, or their surrogates at a local level, performed most services. As a consequence, much of the scholarly and policy debates on democracy at the dawn of the 1990s focused on the need to decentralize and devolve state power to local levels if democratic cultures were to become culturally embedded and to ensure more responsive and effective service delivery by the state. Even though most nation-states in the context of the UN system would pay lip service to this approach, they did very little by way of substantive local reforms to move in the direction of deep decentralization and/or devolution.[1] Apart from the persistent tendency towards centralization, there was also persistent reluctance to adopt participatory mechanisms to make elected leaders and their staff more accountable and connected with ordinary citizens and their organizations.

It is against this backdrop of weak democratic systems, limited commitment to decentralization and participation that the text and approach of the Habitat Agenda needs to be considered. It is therefore understandable that the document is peppered with themes such as 'enablement', 'partnership', 'participation', 'civic engagement', 'solidarity', 'decentralization of authority' and 'capacity building'. The reference to enablement signalled the need for states to formulate and institionalize legal frameworks and fiscal systems that guarantee decentralization, partnerships and participation by civil society and the private sector in local governance processes. Moreover, in the declaration it is strongly asserted that the solution to urbanization characterized by poverty, economic exclusion, slum conditions and negative environmental impacts is indeed sustainable development, which in turn is premissed on democratic governance: 'Democracy, respect for human rights, transparent, representative and accountable government and administration in all sectors of society, as well as effective participation by civil society, are indispensable foundations for the realization of sustainable development.'[2] A few years after Habitat II, the UN–Habitat launched a global campaign to advocate for, and embed, good urban governance.

Global Campaign on Urban Governance

The Global Campaign on Urban Governance (GCUG) is the second part of a twin-track strategy to advance the Habitat Agenda. In the previous chapter I considered at some length the other track, the Global Campaign for Secure Tenure. GCUG is striking for its bold discourse, which comes on the back of a very significant restructuring and repositioning process that UN–Habitat went through in the late 1990s. The outcome of this repositioning exercise was that UN–Habitat resolved to take on more of an advocacy role, presumably because the normal methods of diplomatic policy building proved unsatisfactory or the fact that the urban agenda was simply not achieving traction as a high-profile development issue. The other aspect of the newfound boldness was the explicit poverty-reduction focus underpinned by the principles of equity, urban justice and urban citizenship. These are potentially powerful principles that are suggestive of radical reform.

Flowing from these principles, the campaign sets its sights on the policy ideal of realizing an Inclusive City 'because inclusive decision-making is at the heart of good urban governance'.[3] According to the concept paper, local contexts in cities and towns are always marked by 'the messy reality of competing interests and priorities', and it is therefore essential that the institutions charged with balancing and reconciling competing interests are as inclusive as possible because inclusivity guarantees 'the greatest likelihood for sustainability'.[4] There are a number of conceptual leaps made here which it is important to interrogate more closely, a task I shall return to once I have explained more fully the scaffolding of the concept paper. Now it is important to point out that the paper also stresses the particular importance of including women in urban governance and development processes because they represent the most vulnerable and excluded group alongside older people, youth, the disabled and children. Inclusivity is also located within a rights-based approach to development, which implies an approach to 'poverty reduction based on the full complement of civil, cultural, economic, political and social rights'.[5]

Conceptually, the position paper then moves on to define a range of norms that substantiate what good urban governance means. These are: sustainability, subsidiarity, equity, efficiency, transparency and accountability, civic engagement and citizenship, and security, which are all defined as interdependent and mutually reinforcing. The bulk of the concept paper is then devoted to unpacking each of these principles by spelling out what they may mean if translated into practical actions. In this regard, the objectives are mostly incontestable and the practical measures suggested are indeed far-reaching. Considered differently, if municipalities across the global South implement even half of the objectives and practical measures proposed in the policy paper, it will produce an overnight revolution in local governance in those societies. A wide array of 'cutting edge' urban management reforms are endorsed and promoted by the document: for example, participatory budgeting, full information transparency on the part of governments, quotas for women in local councils because of their systematic disempowerment in most societies, full inheritance rights for women, and so on. Indeed it is hard to quibble with most of the proposed objectives and practical measures.

In particular I want to lift out three of the policy positions which provide an important set of reference points for a radical urban agenda. First, the foregrounding of the urban poor is an important step forward. In most cities in the world, the urban poor remain largely voiceless, excluded from decision-making and usually the biggest sufferers of painful urban reforms, whether in the economy, the environment or the built environment. Also, where local democratization processes are under way, the poor often continue to be excluded, as elites (who straddle political and economic domains) quickly achieve dominance over nominally democratic systems for cultural, historical and economic reasons.[6] Second, the strong emphasis on a comprehensive rights-based approach to development is important because it leads one to a set of political claims that can expose the unequal distribution of resources more clearly, which in turn could serve as a basis for multi-pronged mobilization strategies, including litigation. As we have seen in South Africa and India, where there are strong legal institutions, this can produce important gains for the poor when the state is compelled to address failures in the realization of rights of the poor. Third, the focus on the indivisibility of the various areas of reform is very significant and important to reinforce. Often reluctant states tend to window-dress their democratization efforts with one or two symbolic measures and leave the larger functioning of their economies unreformed. The approach of the policy paper makes it clear that such attempts at policy sophistry are wrong and unacceptable. Finally, the attempt to give concrete expression in terms of practical policy/institutional measures is really valuable for urban coalitions that seek to advance urban transformation through multi-pronged reform campaigns.

However, the policy paper also suffers from a number of serious weaknesses, which may be unavoidable due to the fact that it is a UN document and must by definition find a language and common denominator, or, rather, sophisticated implicitness, that is accommodating of the diverse interests of member countries. Nevertheless, given the influence and mandate of the UN it is equally important to point out the consequences of issues left unsaid or glossed over. The biggest problem with the paper is that it leaves power unexplained and therefore unexposed. There is no explicit line drawn between the conditions the document seeks to remedy and the causal drivers of those conditions. In particular, there is no explanation of why urban exclusion, inequality and systematic dispossession are by and large the norm in most cities of the global South, and, more importantly, of how these conditions persist, often get worse, despite public policies that are nominally pro-poor. This is particularly important because modern forms of rule by postcolonial states rely on justifications (or public discourses) for their actions that may be progressive at the level of formal rhetoric but deeply unjust in terms of the systematic and routine exploitation of the urban poor. Such governing discourses allow the state not only to tolerate but also effectively to facilitate the exploitation of the poor, by failing to regulate elite and private-sector actions effectively. This insidious form of modern rule[7] is one of the most important aspects of urban governance that requires direct engagement if we are to advance the principles promoted by the UN–Habitat concept paper on urban governance.

Another major problem with the concept paper is that it projects too homogenous and uncomplicated a view of the urban poor, as if they are a single category. For instance, when the document argues that 'the ability of the urban poor to influence local decision-making greatly determines the "pro-poorness" of local strategic planning',[8] it obscures the fact that if one does not disaggregate the urban poor in terms of locality, economic positioning, religious and ethnic identity, generation, political sympathies, and so forth, one can design and propagate very bad participatory processes and institutions. In most cities of the global South social life and identities comprised a myriad complex fissure lines and ever-changing moods. Also, poor sectors are marked by a variety of hierarchies and lines of internal exclusion and domination, which can produce 'winners' and 'losers', 'insiders' and 'outsiders', among the poor. Effective governance processes aimed at transforming unequal power relations must be highly sensitive to these dynamics and refrain from constructing the large numbers of urban poor as in any way homogenous or singular.

My last major problem with the concept paper is that it relies heavily on a consensus-based model of urban politics. This is explicitly asserted in the idea that stakeholder forums that bring together the various actors in the city are best placed to 'agree on a broad-based, mission statement and long-term vision for the city, using tools such as strategic planning'. The assumption is that deliberative democratic forums are most likely to facilitate an explicit process of surfacing differences in the city, and through carefully guided processes arrive at agreements on how best to move forward. These assumptions were directly informed by the UN's extensive experimentation and experience with City Consultation processes through the Urban Management Programme (UMP) and the UNEP City Consultations which have been running since the late 1980s. I will briefly focus on the UMP experience because it was more directly influential in shaping the content of the Urban Governance Concept Paper under review. Initially, when it was founded in 1986, UMP simply represented an inter-agency attempt to pool resources and intelligence in various aspects of urban management. This evolved into a focus on 'City and Country Consultations, which [brought] together national and local authorities, the private sector, community representatives, and other stakeholders within a country to discuss specific problems'[9] related to various urban management themes. Later on, after 1996, this was further deepened under the 'Participatory Urban Governance' theme of UMP. In 1999 I carried out a conceptual review of UMP's experiences to distil policy guidelines on advancing participatory urban governance systems and cultures, which took me to the four regions in the World where UMP was anchored (Latin America, the Middle East, South Asia and sub-Saharan Africa).[10] From this review it was clear that stakeholder-based city consultations have become the dominant policy consensus as the more effective mechanism to achieve agreement at city level on the key priorities facing the city, but also to develop so-called action plans that guaranteed that agreements were acted on, by local authorities in particular. This was regarded as the most effective way of achieving participatory democratic cultures and outcomes.

Interestingly, the focus on stakeholder-based, dialogical[11] processes mirrored a trend in Northern cities, where strategic planning became the buzzword from the early 1990s onwards, finding its most celebrated expression in the example of the renewal of Barcelona. On the back of that experience and many others around the world, Jorge Borja and Manuel Castells offered the following definition of urban strategic planning:

> Strategic planning is a way of directing change based on participatory analysis of a situation and its possible evolution and on drawing up of an investment strategy for the scarce resources available at critical points. The diagnosis takes into consideration the settings (globalization), the territory (its various dimensions) and government (or system of public agents). Special consideration is given to dynamics under way, social demands, critical points, obstacles and bottlenecks and potential. The diagnosis is used to determine the foreseeable situation, possible scenarios and desirable situation, which is taken as the starting point for laying down projects to attain it.[12]

Strategic urban planning rests firmly on the foundation of a consensus-based model of urban politics. It is so pervasive and compelling that an entire programme comprising all the big urban development players – the World Bank, UNDP, UN–Habitat, key multilateral donors, and so on – has been established, called Cities Alliance. Their mandate is 'scaling up successful approaches to urban poverty reduction.... By promoting the positive impacts of urbanisation, the Alliance supports learning among cities of all sizes, and also among cities, governments, international development agencies and financial institutions.'[13] Given their level of resources, reach and influence, especially vis-à-vis the Global Good Governance campaign of UN–Habitat, I will devote the second half of the chapter to their conception of urban governance through city development strategies – that is, forms of strategic urban planning. Through this discussion I will elaborate my critique of the consensus-based model of urban politics.

City Development Strategy

City Development Strategy (CDS) emerged to prominence in 2000 as one of four building blocks of the World Bank's new urban and local government policy framework. In this policy framework the following conceptual understanding was put forward to explain what a CDS entails and the link with the World Bank's role in supporting urban development. *Cities in Transition* explains that a CDS is

> a strategy that reflects a broadly shared understanding of the city's socio-economic structure, constraints, and prospects (the analytical assessment) and a *shared* vision of goals, priorities, and requirements (the strategic plan of action). This city development strategy is both a process and a product that identify ways of creating the conditions for urban sustainability along the dimensions of livability, competitiveness, good management and governance, and bankability. ... Each city development strategy exercise would be unique, but all would generally involve three broad phases. A first, 'scoping out' phase would provide a quick assessment of the readiness of the city, the chief concerns of its officials, and the industrial, commercial, and banking interests. These findings would form the basis for a second, more in-depth analysis of the local economic structure and trends, the potential obstacles – institutional, financial, environmental, and social – and the strategic options. A third phase would focus on outside assistance, particularly on how the Bank and other agencies could help the city achieve its goals.[14]

Through a partnership between the World Bank, UN–Habitat and bilateral donors involved in urban development, a new vehicle was created in 1998 to drive two 'action areas: citywide slum upgrading, and the formulation of City Development Strategies. These activities provide support to local capacity to implement the Habitat Agenda and directly attack urban poverty.'[15] In this publication of Cities Alliance, they define CDS in a somewhat different tenor to the World Bank:

> A City Development Strategy is an action-plan for equitable growth in cities, developed and sustained through participation, to improve the quality of life for all citizens. The goals of a City Development Strategy include a collective city vision and action plan aimed at improving urban governance and management, increasing investment to expand employment and services, and systematic and sustained reductions in urban poverty. Achieving this overall goal will occur through a wide variety of approaches in different cities around the world, with local and national conditions determining both the chosen approach and the final outcomes.[16]

It is immediately apparent how the Cities Alliance approach seeks to strike a different chord to the World Bank's blatant primary concern with using CDSs to enhance economic performance and bankability. The Cities Alliance approach foregrounds a concern with poverty reduction and a more inclusive sense of participation compared to the Bank's focus on 'the chief concerns of its [local government] officials, and the industrial, commercial, and banking interests'. However, since the first exposition on CDS by Cities Alliance a much clearer and comprehensive approach was unveiled in 2006 with the publication of *Guide to City Development Strategies: Improving Urban Performance*.[17] Given that Cities Alliance is involved in around 160 cities in the global South with CDS processes, propagating and pursuing the approach of the 2006 document, it is of great relevance to spend some time reviewing its perspective and underlying conceptual assumptions.

The central message of the *Guide to City Development Strategies* is that it is incumbent on all cities to become much more proactive in shaping and directing the future growth and development of their territories. Proactiveness involves: the formulation of a bold but realistic and shared vision for the city; agreement on a limited number of strategic thrusts or priority areas that will be pursued to work systematically towards the vision; and the drafting of an action plan that sets out how, practically, each strategic thrust will be implemented in terms of actors involved, costs and time frames. Getting to a position where CDS forums can identify the right strategic priorities and appropriate responses requires developing a rigorous and up-to-date assessment of the strengths, weaknesses, opportunities and threats (SWOT) that confront the city using a combination of empirical trends data (inclusive of forecasting models) and qualitative information about the 'perceptions' of key actors in the city who are important 'mood shapers'. The data gathered are filtered through a stakeholder forum comprising diverse actors in the city:

> local government (the mayor), the knowledge community (a leading academic in a related policy field), large-scale domestic business (normally the CEO or manager of a leading, fast growing cluster anchor firm), the informal business community (such as the head of the street traders' association or taxi association), the foreign business community (the manager of one of the leading multinationals anchoring a cluster), public health and the environment, and labour (or workers' association).[18]

Critically, one of the governance issues that must be understood is that the CDS is the product of a forum that exceeds local government, and its vision, strategies and action plans pertain to all the stakeholders involved. It is therefore not a tool that sets out the role and actions of local government but rather one that seeks to complement, inform and guide the administrative and urban management institutional mechanisms of local government such as spatial plans, annualized strategic plans, sectoral plans for transport, education, health and so forth. This is an important issue, to which I will return later.

The underlying policy idea is that in a highly competitive and increasingly integrated global economy it is vital for all cities to adopt a razor-sharp strategy about how best to position their territory in that context in order to minimize negative impacts, anticipate potential shocks, and exploit comparative and competitive potential. Given the nature of urban governments in most parts of the developing world, marked by inefficient and overly bureaucratic structures with limited resources and powers, the idea of a deliberate, proactive strategy is a far-reaching proposition. Furthermore, given that democratic cultures and institutions are not very well developed or effective, the core idea of a CDS being a co-created process and product is also significant. Lastly, the insistence that the strategy must explicitly address the imperatives of poverty reduction and environmental health represents a significant challenge for most local governments, which tend to prioritize the needs of elites and middle classes, who are perceived to be the main drivers of local wealth and prosperity – that is, the tax base of local government. The most recent exposition on CDS by Cities Alliance represents an important policy shift as strategic planning methodologies are combined with a pro-poor discourse, linked to environmental concerns, and underpinned by the imperatives of achieving sustained economic growth in a globalizing economy.

Looking back to the first expositions on CDS in the late 1990s and the more recent work available on the Cities Alliance website, it is apparent that an ideal-type CDS process rests on the following three assumptions, among others:

• A shared vision of the future is definable through deliberation and negotiation between various, preferably all, stakeholders and such a 'consensus vision' can serve as a basis to inform choices about trade-offs, alignment and investment of scarce public and private resources.

- A well-structured process (inclusive and rigorous) of dialogue will lead to an outcome that is the sum total of the best possible 'rational consensus' about the nature of problems and what needs to be done to address them.

- The diverse and wide-ranging challenges facing the city are knowable, intelligible and can be broken down into discrete parcels of knowledge to inform targeted interventions or interventions.

I will now engage in a closer reading of the *Guide to City Development Strategies* document because it reflects the core of the contemporary 'progressive' mainstream consensus about how to address simultaneously growth, poverty reduction, environmental health and political inclusion. Put differently, the CDS approach is regarded as the surest route to the realization of the normative principles and development ideals of the good urban governance agenda discussed earlier in the chapter. More importantly, CDSs are spreading like wildfire across cities in the global South and therefore represent a critical site of contestation about how to organize democratic engagement and policy debate about the deep challenges associated with rapid and differential urbanization. Given the vast scope of the *Guide to City Development Strategy*, I will explore three central issues: the potential and problems of dialogical forums, which hold the integrity of CDS; the conception of drivers of economic performance in terms of inclusivity/exclusivity; and the prospects of a holistic and balanced developmental outcome if the model is adopted. Given the overall focus of this chapter, I devote most of the following discussion to the first of these three issues.

Dialogical forums and democratic quality

The widespread assumption in most urban governance models at the moment is that participatory processes are a prerequisite for more legitimate and relevant policy processes and outcomes. This position finds expression in the idea of a CDS forum in the *Guide* document. The role of the CDS Forum is principally to define the vision, process the data that arise from the SWOT analysis, and come to an agreement on the strategic priorities that arise from such an analysis. The *Guide* document also provides a series of guiding questions on five thematic areas that will invariably arise in such a strategic review processes: 'Livelihood, such as job creation, business development, and sources of household income; Environmental sustainability and energy efficiency of the city and the quality of its service delivery; Spatial form and its infrastructure; Financial resources; and, Governance.'[19]

Two issues are immediately important from a participatory democratic point of view: the composition of this group and the influence of their decisions on the daily workings of local government, which is subjected to more rigorous democratic oversight instruments compared to corporatist forums.[20] It is important to recall that a CDS is not meant to be a local government plan or strategy but rather a co-crafted and co-owned strategy that sits between local government, the business community, including representatives of informal trading associations, civil society organizations and academia. The imperative is to achieve consensus and buy-in across the key sectors and fissures of the city in order to focus energies and achieve the benefits that potentially arise from joint action. Consensus also helps to eliminate unnecessary inefficiencies and can lead to joint action to remove obstacles to growth, economic inclusion, and so forth. However, in the *Guide* document there is an overriding pragmatism to make sure that the CDS process is as quick as possible to avoid a loss of momentum and interest. Thus, it envisages a relatively small CDS Stakeholder Forum on the assumption that the participants have good linkages back to their constituencies and come into the process with strong mandates and/or a clear perspective on what the views of their stakeholder groups are. This is how the document envisions the scope and form of participation:

> It is expected that each member of the stakeholder committee will be truly representative of a large network of the people of the city and reflects their concerns. If the group is larger than 10, it is too large and will tend to be ineffective in dealmaking, as well as being too unwieldy to convene. The CDS process is essentially based on collaborative planning; extensive literature on collaborative planning indicates the need for small-group strategic development, with carefully chosen members

who truly reflect their constituencies and can speak and bargain on behalf of these constituencies.[21]

The obvious question that arises is: who determines who gets 'carefully chosen' and makes the judgement call that the chosen indeed 'truly reflect their constituencies'? Also, many more fundamental questions are left unaddressed. For example, if this burst of work is not subjected to the normal, even if highly unsatisfactory, checks and balances of democratic systems within local government, how much influence is it allowed to have over the budgetary allocations of the municipality, which arguably is subject to the oversight mechanisms of a representative democratic system? This is not a trivial question because if one considers the vast array of infrastructure, economic, settlement and spatial issues prioritized through the CDS process, it is clear that if the CDS is to be successful, it will essentially colonize and direct public expenditure that sits in municipal, provincial/regional and national budgets that deal with key infrastructures of the urban built environment. In light of this, and the normative principles embedded in the good governance campaign of UN–Habitat campaign discussed earlier, there is potential slippage here that can do great harm to the agenda of participatory governance.

To underscore this critique I want to turn briefly to the very literature on 'collaborative planning' that the *Guide* purports to take as its inspiration and guidance. Through this literature it becomes apparent that the democratic benchmark for multi-stakeholder deliberation is rather higher than intimated by Cities Alliance. The rise of strategic planning, initially mainly in Northern cities, runs in tandem with the theoretical discourse on collaborative planning. It is in the context of institutionalizing strategic planning that stakeholder-based dialogical forums have come to the fore. As mentioned earlier, for Jorge Borja and Manuel Castells strategic planning can only be successful if it involves a wide spectrum of stakeholders from various backgrounds in the city: 'Strategic planning is a way of directing change based on a participatory analysis of a situation and its possible evolution', and further achieves beyond everything else 'the dissemination of strategic thought, the process being more important than the results themselves'. Crucially, the 'participation of the public and private agents is an indispensable condition of strategic planning and distinguishes it from other forms of planning'.[22] This has obviously been taken up by the mainstream consensus embodied in the policy frameworks of Cities Alliance and UN–Habitat. However, it is the communicative planning school of thought (and their critics) that have gone furthest in theorizing the political implications of this approach to urban planning and its reliance on stakeholder-based participation mechanisms.

According to the communicative planning school of thought, dialogical processes are effectively structured mechanisms to surface and confront the 'dilemmas as regards co-existence in shared spaces'.[23] The assumption is that the city is composed of a rich diversity of social actors (with diverse interests and divergent senses of place), rooted in multiple and disjunctive territories, with often divergent claims. This diversity, along with the multiplicity of exogenous and endogenous forces that impinge on urban development, produces a profoundly complex array of challenges. Therefore, for Patsy Healey, this approach rests on

> a dynamic relational view of urban life. Its focus is on relations and processes, not objects. It emphasizes dynamics not statics, and the complex interactions between local continuities and 'social capital' and the innovative potential. It 'sees' multiple relations transecting the space of the city, each 'driven' and 'shaped' by different forces, interacting with each other in different ways, bypassing, conflicting, coordinating in complex trajectories. It recognizes that these social relationships, although shaped by powerful forces, often outside the space of a particular urban areas, are actively socially constructed. In the social processes of defining meanings and identities and in the routine ways of living in the city, people make the multiple times and places, its differentiations, cohesions and exclusions, and its power dynamics.[24]

It is important to remember that this dynamic, shifting and complex reality of cities is much more intense in the global South because of the coexistence of formal and informal cities at scales that dwarf the challenges of Northern cities, as demonstrated in Chapter 2. In view of this constitutive 'multiplexity', as Healey prefers to call it, the following rationale underpins the need for dialogical governance and planning mechanisms. By definition such complexity in the city can only be addressed through *synectics* – an approach to solving problems based on creative thinking of a group from different areas of expertise and knowledge. Therefore, it follows that in order to forge sustainable economic, political and social ecologies for cities it is essential that these diverse social actors confront each other with their divergent claims in order to arrive at difficult, politically situated, decisions about whose claims will be addressed, in what sequence and with what resources. Since assent and compliance depend on the legitimacy and inclusivity of the process, it is essential that as many stakeholders as possible participate in such dialogical forums. Further on, communicative theorists assert that it is not impossible to arrive at legitimate, contextually situated agreements without some measure of shared values, which ideally can be expressed through a shared vision about the future.[25] However, in a context of deep social cleavages and structural inequalities it is not that easy to arrive at shared values, or to come to an agreement that is real and broad enough to incorporate the interests of both the urban elites and the urban poor, 'encroachers' and 'informals', especially since these categories are shot through with very profound lines of differentiation and even inequality. Clearly, the idea that one can satisfy the requirements of meaningful consensus-building forums through the methodology proposed by Cities Alliance is difficult to sustain. However, to illustrate properly the political (legitimacy) problems with the methodological approach in democratic terms, it is instructive to explore how the challenge of economic growth and inclusion is handled in the CDS framework.

Drivers of economic performance

The basic argument of the *Guide* is that cities must pay a lot more explicit attention to how they are going to grow their economies 'sustainably' and achieve a much higher degree of economic inclusion as growth takes off. The latter question is approached through the lens of livelihoods and leads to a policy emphasis on the poor health, education and limited livelihood options of the urban poor. Growth is tied to competitiveness, which in turn is linked to 'business climate'. One of the major instruments to drive both equity concerns and economic growth is of course infrastructure investment. The *Guide* asserts that:

Infrastructure assessment and investment planning are complex and require careful attention in CDS processes. Often, tradeoffs are required (and synergies may exist) between equity objectives (providing basic services to all members of urban society at affordable rates) and economic objectives, which may be facilitated by expressways, ports, airports, and so on.[26]

This assertion demonstrates the point made earlier that the strategies that arise from the CDS Forum are meant to impact on public expenditure in a major way, but it also hints at the trade-offs that must be made in deciding how to ensure economic competitiveness. Such an analysis is inherently ideological and politically contested because it is not clear how to pursue a growth path within the parameters of the neoliberal global economic order and realize poverty-reduction objectives at the same time; a profound dilemma that is effectively glossed over in the *Guide to City Development Strategies* document.

For example, in *Splintering Urbanism* the evidence is overwhelming that network infrastructures – transport, telecommunications, energy, water and streets – privileged in the current global economic climate demand of cities the prioritizing of the connectivity systems of high-end service and manufacturing sectors, as well as the security and mobility needs of the middle class and elites.[27] Thus, large chunks of capital investment go into expressways, ports, airports, telecommunications networks, and the like, squeezing out investment in more mundane infrastructure that could dramatically improve the quality of life of the urban poor disconnected from basic services or underinvested health and education systems. This sense of economic infrastructure prioritization is simply reinforced when the *Guide* suggests that cities need to 'benchmark' themselves against comparable, competitor and aspirational cities – that is, cities in the race to take the lead on satisfying the ferocious appetites of particular economic sectors which tend to skew the investment priorities of cities away from the poor. The analysis of UN–Habitat in its 2001 *Global Report on Human Settlements* speaks most directly to this issue in their discussion of the uneven distribution of the benefits and costs of globalization. The UN–Habitat report[28] explains how a 'hyperglobalist' view of globalization has come to dominate policy discourses, which leads to a particular way of thinking about the role of cities:

Those holding this view ... tend to believe that the increasing globalization of the economy is inevitable. They also consider globalization as
beneficial and that it will eventually have advantages all over the world
... In this scenario, the nation state is seen as losing its role in a world
that chiefly involves interactions between transnational business and
city or regional governance. Economic globalization is seen as a natural
process and city governments should ensure that its citizens derive the
maximum benefit from it. Cities should adapt their policies to conform
to the imperatives that the process demands.[29]

Due to the existing conditions of widespread urban poverty and
inequality, the UN–Habitat report suggests that the hyperglobalization approach to the role of city governments in mediating economic
development dynamics will further exacerbate the problem. Furthermore, the report notes, it tends to produce governance cultures within
which economic interests become decisive in decision-making with
regard to urban planning and management priorities. In this environment, city visions can be dangerous things when business-dominated
growth coalitions in the city use strategic planning processes to push
policies that will attract foreign investment. 'The aim is to ensure that
this vision [for the future of the city] informs other policies of the
city, including the strategic land use plan, and expenditure priorities.'[30]
Given the simplistic, or rather apolitical, way in which the dynamics
surrounding prioritization of urban policies are discussed in the Cities
Alliance *Guide* document it is difficult to avoid the conclusion that
it reinforces a hyperglobalization approach to urban competitiveness
imperatives, despite the reference to balancing competitiveness with
poverty reduction and environmental health concerns. What is missing
is a more rigorous political economy assessment of the obstacles that
stand in the way of a deep, probably conflictual, strategic dialogue
between not only diverse but fundamentally opposite interests in
the city. The facile promotion of small (no more than ten), mobile,
rapid deliberation forums to define and drive a CDS is a recipe for
political manipulation by the powerful, which could, if successful,
fundamentally skew the priorities of municipalities, which would then
take their cue for their infrastructure budgets from the vision and
strategic argument of the CDS forum. When the ideas of 'small' and
'rapid' gets combined with equally simplistic notions that 'tradeoffs,
as well as synergies, exist between equity objectives (providing basic

services to all members of society at affordable rates) and economic objectives (which may be facilitated by expressways, ports, airports and the like)',[31] the likelihood of transformative CDS outcomes (in the form promoted by Cities Alliance) becomes far-fetched.

Prospects of holistic development outcomes

It is irrefutable that the *Guide to City Development Strategies* strives to help city governments to use strategic planning tools and dialogical forums to formulate tailor-made strategies that will effectively define and deliberate the trade-offs that need to be made in the short and medium term regarding investment decisions and service standards (and prices) to achieve a locally defined vision. What the preceding discussion suggests is that the methodology proposed by the CDS is deeply flawed because of the lack of an explicit treatment of the power dynamics that underpin city politics and ultimately structure governance relations. For instance, local governments are treated in the document almost as blank institutions that can simply change course and adopt a new approach to urban planning, management and co-governance, as if their existing functioning is not steeped in profound historical, cultural and economic systems which shape an incentive architecture that serves to reproduce the system. Trade-offs between equity and competitiveness are proposed as if they are genuine and not predefined by a powerful set of discourses about becoming 'modern', 'world class', 'globally connected'; discourses that make certain interests and groups appear rational or irrational, reasonable or radical, and so forth. Discursive terrains in cities make it possible for particular kinds of voices and interest groups to be seen and recognized (as I will demonstrate more clearly in the next chapter) and therefore considered acceptable to participate in deliberations about priorities and the terms of negotiation that underpin so-called trade-offs.

To illustrate the difficulty of conducting 'real', 'hard' and largely conflictual debate on the city, it is useful to diagrammatize the different categories of decisions that need to be made in the course of urban planning and management processes. Figure 4.1 differentiates between three categories of public investment: household, economic and public. Household infrastructure refers to basic services such as

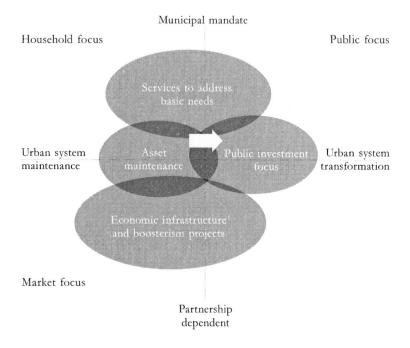

FIGURE 4.1   Municipal priorities and trade-offs[32]

water, waste, sanitation and electricity, which come either bundled with low-cost housing or *in situ* upgrading programmes. Economic infrastructure refers primarily to network infrastructures such as transport, telecommunications, energy, water and streets, which are built to enhance the economic desirability and functionality of the city. The form, quality and extensiveness of these infrastructures are driven by global expectations of transnational businesses that are lured to invest in particular city regions. Lastly, public infrastructure includes: public transport, public spaces, urban accessibility through equitable land markets, public health, environment, social–cultural facilities to pursue and enhance identity, and so forth. Furthermore, the existing built infrastructures require ongoing maintenance and renewal, which can be defined as a further pole in the matrix of prioritization. At any point in time in the (political) life of city governance, trade-offs are made in relation to the size of the budget of the municipality and what is deemed to be politically important. In the current global climate, the tendency is emphatically to invest heavily in the economic attractiveness of cities, which implies large-scale investment in economic infrastructure and a serious of boosterism projects such as sports stadiums, art galleries (such as the Guggenheim Musuem in Bilbao), signature architectural buildings, all of which undoubtedly crowd out and undermine pro-poor spending and investment in public infrastructures that serve everyone in the city. The interests that maintain this conception of political pragmatism are pervasive and deeply entrenched and unlikely to be dislodged by the facile conception of trade-offs embodied in the CDS *Guide* of Cities Alliance. This is a large claim on my part, which is why the next chapter is devoted to a detailed conceptual elaboration of how to think about urban politics and radical transformation.

5

Reconceptualizing the political
in cities

Without transgression, without the red boundary, there is no danger,
no risk, no *frisson*, no experiment, no discovery and no creativity.
Without extending some hidden or visible frontier of the possible,
without disturbing something of the incomplete order of things
there is no challenge, no pleasure, and certainly no joy.[1]

Limitations are ... conditions of possibility. However, to accept
given limitations as that which determines all that is possible would
make being unbearably heavy. Limits are truly enabling when, having
given something its form, ... the form engages with its own limits
to fashion its own style. Foucault's notion of transgression signifies
work on *enabling* limits.[2]

In light of my repeated criticism of mainstream policies and argument that the true nature of differential power inequalities in cities
is under-specified and under-theorized, it is important to lay bare
the reasons for my critique and what an alternative approach could
look like. In this chapter I adopt a more conceptual tone to clarify
the theoretical strands that feed into an embracing of radical democracy as the most useful and productive approach to urban politics,
which always boil down to complex and profound trade-offs between
competing priorities, as argued in the previous chapter. Furthermore,
if progressive actors in cities are to position themselves not only
to critique but also present alternative ways of thinking about and

intervening in cities, it is imperative that they do so with a razor-sharp perspective on political landscapes and opportunities. In this sense, this central chapter is a vital foundation stone for the propositional and policy-oriented chapters that follow, particularly Chapters 7 and 8. This chapter starts off with a distillation of seven theoretical premisses that inform the theoretical framework for urban politics which I introduced at the outset. The remainder of the chapters offer a more detailed discussion of that framework, defined as a relational model of urban politics. The informing sensibility of this chapter is the evocative idea of transgression at the edge of mainstream consensus in order to subvert and remould new and more empowering agreements on sustainable forms of city building.

Conceptual premisses

The conceptual model that follows draws on a variety of recent theorizations in urban studies, political science, policy studies, urban planning and development studies. The common denominator is a concern with culture as constitutive of the social, alongside the economic and political. With the cultural turn in urban theory, and social theory more broadly, comes an awareness that language, discourse and symbolic meanings are central to the incessant processes of identity construction and the realm of agency in the spaces of the everyday. Conceptually, the challenge is to adopt an approach that recognizes the structuring effect of the economy, bureaucracy and discursive diagrams of power without relinquishing an appreciation of agency.[3] The following conceptual reference points fall squarely within this tradition of theorization and serve as a foundation for the alternative approach to urban politics that I propose in the next section. Due to space constraints it is unavoidably abbreviated and at best suggestive.

1. Urban politics must be imagined, practised and institutionalized on an ethical basis. Ideally, this is a human-rights-based framework that legally guarantees access to opportunities to flourish as a creative individual ensconced in multiple communities of affinity, which may or may not be in close proximity.[4] For example, in South Africa, a strong basis for such an approach exists due to

the constitutional entrenchment of all human rights – political, civil and socio-economic – and it is of course also endorsed in the good urban governance campaign of UN–Habitat. It is vital to maximize this political potential in all spheres of citizenship and political practice.

2. Democracy is a necessary precondition for a vibrant political space that allows for regulated contestation of perspectives that are invariably imbued with particular interests. Formal liberal democratic norms and institutional procedures that rest on representative democratic institutions and the rule of law are inadequate to address the structurally embedded relations and systems of inequality that characterize capitalist modernity.[5] More is needed. In this regard, the ideas of scholars who espouse the benefits of radical democracy are the most convincing and promising.[6] More on the institutional expressions of radical democracy will be explored below.

3. The institutional design and functioning dimensions of urban politics are crucial for the effectiveness and democratic content of political practices. Institutions are not merely containers of political intent, but rather mediate in a fundamental sense how interactions between diverse political actors (and agendas) are structured and channelled.[7] This awareness brings into view the importance of organizational dynamics and cultures of both state and non-state political actors, but also the importance of translating new political agreements into 'the routine practices of frontline officials [in government] if they are to make real differences to people's life chances and to give real respect to people's individual life circumstances'.[8] In many ways, the conceptual model put forward in this chapter adds up to an attempt to illuminate the institutional interdependencies between various political domains in the city.

4. The conceptual distinctions between 'government', 'governmentality' and 'governance' are useful to understand and recast the potential and limitations of the local state, especially in an era of neoliberal dominance. In my usage, 'government' refers in practical terms to the structures, institutions and organizations of the state that regulate social practices.[9] 'Governmentality' is a Foucauldian

concept which refers to 'the complex array of techniques – programs, procedures, strategies and tactics – employed by both non-state administrative agencies and state institutions to shape conduct of individuals and populations'.[10] Governance denotes the relationality of power as it flows through networks between the state and institutional actors in the market and civil society. However, 'governance is not a homogenous agent, but a morass of complex networks and arenas within which power dynamics are expressed and deployed'.[11] The purpose of this alternative conceptual model is to bring these multiple networks and arenas of urban governance into view so that more fine-grained critical research can be conducted. I also hope to provoke investigations into practicable visions about radical politics that can produce more socially just and environmentally conscious outcomes – that is, political discourses that emerge from practical struggles to test and transcend the discursive limits of governmentality practices of the state.

5. The full measure of the urban political terrain can only be apprehended via an appreciation of spatiality. Cities can be understood spatially in terms of densities, proximities, intensities and their effects. Furthermore, the particular form of the spatial configuration that arises in a city shapes the horizons of possibility.[12] If the horizon is extremely limited, spatial configuration continues to produce segregation, fragmentation and exclusion. Alternatively, if the horizons are more open, we are more inclined to use the rich multiplicity of spatial practices to unleash new ways of interaction and engagement. However, if the multiple spatialities of the city are repressed or erased (in official texts and regulations), it is virtually impossible to construct a radical democratic 'cosmopolis', in the parlance of radical planner Leonie Sandercock. In other words, recognition of the inherently heterogeneous time-spaces of the city feeds into political questions about how the city is imagined and represented. At its core, all urban struggles are in one sense or another about the politics of recognition and determination of identity.

6. This 'multiplex' perspective of the city rests firmly on a non-essentialist conception of identity and community. Kian Tajbakhsh

explains that 'identities are not expressive of a deep "essentialist" core, but are best seen as contingent and articulated through interdependent and overdetermined practices structured by both conscious intention and unconscious desire.' In other words, 'complexity is the *a piori* feature of social identity'.[13] Invariably the same applies to the notion of 'community'. Frances Cleaver (among many others) has successfully demonstrated how '"community" in participatory approaches to development is often seen as a "natural" social entity characterized by solidaristic relations.'[14] She then goes on to critique this approach systematically, by pointing out the absence of 'coterminosity between natural (resource), social and administrative boundaries'.[15] Furthermore, she points out how processes of conflict, negotiation, inclusion and exclusion have been poorly analysed in the development literature, with a tendency to romanticize community relations. This has arguably become worse with the rise of social capital literature during the past decade. The same argument can then be extended to the notion of the 'urban poor', which is often used interchangeably with 'community'. Earlier I highlighted why homogenizing the urban poor is dangerous and conceptually problematic.

7. Finally, it is important to acknowledge that political contestation unfolds around specific, discursively constructed, points of crisis and imperatives to reproduce the political economic system. What is regarded as a *crisis* and finds its way into the public domain via the media is an important area of contestation. Representative democracy, collective and insurgent practices of poor classes, and mundane practices to realize development projects rely on the public recognition of certain issues as valid political problems. Usually this is reflected in the discourses that circulate in (popular) media via newspapers, radio, television and, increasingly, cyberspace. More and more, successful political mobilization of interests relies on capacity to set the agenda and frame the issues of the day. This point brings me back to my first assertion about the importance of an ethical horizon in political engagement. It seems clear that the potentiality of a rights-based discourse can only be realized through practical struggles that translate everyday violations into claims, demands, remedies and solutions

that find recognition and expression in the public domain. In other words, politics is mainly about substantive content, but is also about performance. The question is, how does one reimagine political agency at a subjective and collective level in ways that can transcend governmentality through performative practices in *all* domains of political action? Hopefully, the conceptual model elaborated in the next section will serve as a suitable starting point to answering this question.

Sketches of a conceptual model of urban politics

This section is the heart of the chapter and the book. Here the aim is to capture the multiple, interconnected and overlapping spaces of political practices in the city. As proposed in Chapter 1, in conceptual terms it is possible to delineate at least five domains of

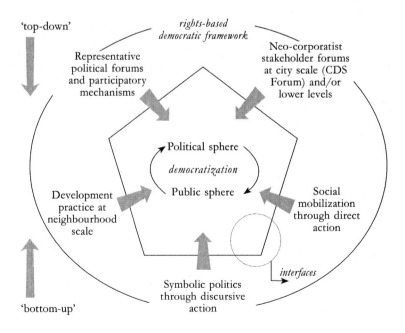

FIGURE 5.1 Domains of political engagement in the relational city

political engagement between the state, the private sector and civil society at various scales, ranging from the global and national to the local: (1) representative political forums and associated participatory mechanisms; (2) neo-corporatist political forums such as the ones that develop city development strategies, which comprise representative organizations, typically the government, the private sector, trade unions and community-based organizations; (3) direct action or mobilization against state policies or to advance specific political demands; (4) the politics of development practice, especially at the grassroots; and (5) symbolic political contestation as expressed through discursive contestation in the public sphere. Figure 5.1 depicts these five political domains in addition to distinctions between the political and public spheres that are continuously (re)constructed through engagement in each of these five spheres and their interfaces.

The value of this exercise is that it allows one to rethink political practice from multiple angles. Moreover, it opens up new ground for imagining more creative progressive political strategies to undermine and subvert the oppressive functioning of dominant interests in the city. The model rests heavily on Foucault's understanding of power and therefore locates discursive and symbolic dimensions of political practice as central to re-reading political institutions and agency.[16] I will briefly elaborate each domain in terms of key defining features, types of political practices, inter-connections with other domains and possible pitfalls.

Domain one: representative politics

Political representation refers to the formal political system that characterizes national, provincial/regional and municipal government. At all levels, the main avenue of political participation in this process is through political parties that are elected. The democratic effectiveness of electoral systems depends in large measure on the democratic nature of the respective political parties along with their rootedness in their constituencies.[17] It also depends on the quality and maturity of the institutional rules and systems that structure the functioning of political chambers, council and committee meetings, and associated mechanisms for transparency, responsiveness and accountability.

The policy framework in the UN–Habitat concept paper on urban governance provides a solid foundation for participatory local governance where the full diversity and conflictual interests of the city can be expressed. Naturally this depends on 'political commitment' to formulate more practical policies to create various participatory governance mechanisms such as citizen juries, participatory budget councils, integrated development planning forums, area-based political committees, citizen opinion surveys, participatory action research studies to test policy preferences and options, transparency guidelines and support systems, and so forth.[18] Beyond political commitment, it also depends on the tangible accountability of the elected politicians.

The literatures on urban regimes, growth coalitions and elite pacts demonstrate the subtle and blatant ways in which (organized) business interests that rely on public investment frameworks and spending (for transport, land-use zoning and preparation, environmental guidelines, etc.), exert their influence over the decision-making and functioning of local government.[19] If one approaches participatory instruments with a naivety about these relations they easily become a camouflage for what is really going on in the city. The point about participatory local governance is to increase the democratic oversight of active citizens, especially those whose human rights are systematically denied due to inadequate services and lack of opportunities. However, this is unlikely to take root unless citizens are well organized, and are supported by municipal government to organize themselves actively into independent and articulate voices.[20] These qualifiers point to the importance of the political values and practices of the political parties that hold majority power in the council. Even though it is a neglected subject in the literature, it is clear that the democratic culture – open or closed – within political parties is a vital aspect in embedding meaningful participatory local governance.

I began with a discussion of the representative domain of political practice because it is in this domain that an enabling climate can be constructed for the flourishing of political agency in other domains of social action. This is why the reforms advocated for through the Good Urban Governance Campaign are so important but also dangerous if left undertheorized in terms of power relations in the city. Specifically, municipal government (with visionary leaders) is an important

precursor for the establishment of 'neo-corporatist' forums to undertake strategic planning regarding the future trajectory of the city. In
fact, close synergy between the municipal development policies and the
broader CDS that emerges from multi-stakeholder governance forums
is essential. However, given the built-in bias towards more organized,
well-resourced and articulate voices in multi-stakeholder forums, the
elected politicians have a vital role to play in ensuring that marginal
and poorly organized interests in the city, who should be the primary
beneficiaries of the developmental local government mandate, can also
find their issues infused in the deliberations. There are few guarantees
that this is likely to happen, but this does not negate the conceptual
assertion. When I elaborate on autonomous agency by marginal and
poor classes and groups below it will become clearer that I locate this
conceptual assertion within a larger theoretical diagram of agonistic,
conflict-ridden contestation between various political agendas in the
city. Seen from that position, it is legitimate to invoke the democratic
expectation about the ideal role of elected politicians.

There are many other dangers when it comes to the functioning
of representative politics, which underscore the danger of vesting all
hope for radical democracy in the emergence of effective representative democratic institutions. Much more is required, as the remainder
of the chapter will demonstrate.

Domain two: neo-corporatist stakeholder forums

Stakeholder-based forums refer to formal deliberative institutions
that provide a regulated and predictable space for negotiation and
contestation between state, civil society and private-sector representative organizations on urban issues of (mutual) concern, even if for
different reasons. Commonly they are referred to as multi-stakeholder
forums. In their book *Local and Global*, Jorge Borja and Manuel Castells
set out the case for the necessity of these kinds of deliberative spaces
to co-create strategic plans for the city.[21] They frame their argument
against the backdrop of the impact of globalization processes on
cities. Such impacts make it more important than ever that public
infrastructure investments (especially transport and communication)
are carefully made in terms of a larger strategic vision of where the
urban economy is headed. By definition, such a vision cannot be

the fabrication of municipal planners but must arise from properly structured processes of participation and deliberation, because it must not only be viable but also politically embedded among the diverse stakeholders in the city. Without legitimacy, strategic plans are bound to run aground on the banks of political conflict and corruption. The perspective of Borja and Castells clearly operates on a shift away from master planning to strategic planning to accommodate the complexity of urban life. It also builds on the strong participatory thrust that propels discourses on greater decentralization and deliberative democracy. This is an orientation that is echoed in the literature on city development strategies by the Cities Alliance.

Earlier, in reflecting on the city development strategy tenets of the Cities Alliance, I summarized the various lines of critique that can levelled against it. However, before one becomes completely dismissive of these arenas of political engagement it is worthwhile to remember that the stakeholder forum mechanism was key to the political resolution of the South African crisis of apartheid in the early 1990s. At the dawn of the South African transition process (in the late 1980s), a number of negotiation forums started to emerge at a local level as white municipalities entered into negotiations to end or circumvent rates- and service-charge boycotts.[22] These institutional forms became somewhat paradigmatic throughout the transition because they provided a model which allowed oppositional political organizations to retain their relative autonomy whilst renegotiating the terms of their relationship as the process of democratization shifted power to the black majority and their representative organizations (former political liberation movements such as the African National Congress, the Pan-Africanist Congress and the like). In other words, the forums provided a guarantee against unilateral decisions that would radically alter economic and political relations in society. It is for this reason that many regard them as reformist corporatist institutions that simply serve to entrench vested elite interests by diffusing militant social action by subjugated classes.[23]

Should these criticisms lead us to reject the role of multi-stakeholder forums in advancing radical democratic urban politics? I think not. It is crucial to remain aware of the depoliticizing dangers of such forums, along with the built-in tendency to cater for well-organized,

well-resourced and articulate political groups. Yet, given the complexity of urban development challenges it is imperative to build
broad-based agreement, even if provisional and continuously renewed,
about the future direction of the city. The obligations entrenched in
the UN–Habitat Agenda to progressively realize everyone's socio-
economic rights must be the touchstone for the institutional rules
and agenda of such forums. In other words, in terms of institutional
design and functioning, provision must be made for ensuring adequate
representation of potentially marginalized groups and ensuring that
the search for consensus does not rule out the necessity of agonistic
engagement. The work of Michael Gunder and Jean Hillier, among
others, points to a series of useful principles that can be used to
ensure fair and critical deliberation, which does not preclude non-
institutionalized direct action or opting to exit.[24]

However, the progressive potential of these mechanisms can only
be secured if civil society actors maintain their autonomy and actively
pursue political strategies that unfold in spheres of engagement and
communication outside of the chambers of stakeholder forums. The
leverage power of groups in forums representing the interests of the
poor and future generations will be dependent on the power of such
constituencies in the public sphere, in particular the power that comes
from direct action to shape agendas and lay claim to constitutionally
defined rights and entitlements. Furthermore, strong social organization at the grassroots potentially strengthens the accountability of
elected politicians. This relational dynamic can be harnessed to ensure
that conservative agendas that will further exploit the poor become
inconceivable for the political class. The multi-stakeholder forums can
then become discursive spaces where a more redistributive 'consensus'
can be constructed and consolidated. The fact is that unless business
interests and the middle classes are publicly and incessantly compelled
to ascribe to the importance of redistribution, it is virtually impossible
to use local-government service provision and taxation as effective
tools to achieve greater equity in the city. Multi-stakeholder forums
can be important sites of contestation and engagement to socially
construct such political agreements. This is dependent on the social
power of the poor and other marginal groups established through
effective organization and mobilization around everyday struggles.

It is also dependent on the circulation of alternative discourses and substantiating knowledge that demonstrates how distributive justice can work to the benefit of all citizens in the city. As stressed earlier, it is crucial to appreciate the *relational* interdependency between various domains of political practice.

Domain three: direct action

Direct action involves various forms of collective action by (disadvantaged) groups aimed at stretching the liberal democratic constitutional framework to its limit.[25] This implies that social movements and looser, issue-specific, social groups must claim their rights and entitlements through non-violent social action focused on concrete issues that shape the quality of life of their constituencies. In a sense, the primary function of progressive direct action is to maintain political momentum for redistribution and realization of human rights, especially socio-economic rights. Of all the political practices in the city, this type pushes most blatantly at the boundaries of the possible (in discursive, political and juridical terms). Direct action seeks to disturb the tranquillity of 'business as usual', whereby local governance unfolds at arm's length from the citizenry and politicians nestle snugly in the bosom of elites. It potentially shakes up the middle-class lack of interest in life beyond the suburb – that is, livelihood challenges in the slums and other spaces of marginalization. Street conflicts, clashes and destabilizations that spark off direct action are prerequisites for political agreements to address urban inequalities. Such agreements will invariably involve attitudinal and behavioural change among the middle classes, because they will have to fund more aggressive redistribution and more effective government. (Not that their financial contributions are proportionately more significant than those the poor already contribute simply to survive, despite inadequate support from the state.)

To be sure, direct action is not about consensus. Invariably, it raises the political temperature and solicits conflict from those who stand to lose if demands are acceded to. From an agonistic political perspective such conflict is necessary to combust crisis, which in turn can produce political engagement and provisional agreements between opponents to allow governance and management to carry on. The challenge is to foster a political culture that is embracing of social mobilization politics along with institutionally defined pressure-valves to absorb and channel the energy unleashed by direct action. Participatory mechanisms associated with representative political domains can be useful mediating channels to ensure that the demands of claimants are articulated to actual plans, agendas and budgets of local government as requisite in terms of annual and medium-term planning processes. Similarly, task teams that undertake the work of multi-stakeholder forums can expand their deliberations to address the claims and issues of those on the streets. The oft-forgotten relational dynamic of urban politics comes to the fore yet again.

In this light I am often frustrated with radical proposals for urban politics that simply call for the poor to rise up and militantly refuse to accept their conditions but then say nothing about what happens when such claims are potentially acceded to, for any political gain must be institutionalized in some form to be enduring and comprehensively adhered to. In other words, my conceptualization rejects social mobilization for the sake of it – that is, militancy without a purpose, without a potentially winnable demand. For example, it remains unclear whether the recent wave of social protests in many South African cities are merely reactive or premissed on a clear strategy to articulate the diverse domains of political practice in the city. Hard, ideologically pure rhetoric tends to militate against reflexive and adaptive political strategy. Such rhetoric is impervious to strategic, contingent political praxis.

Collective action through embodied public displays of protest, celebration, defiance, or whatever, is not inherently progressive or conservative. In my view, progressive direct action is marked by the political philosophy and agenda of the movement and, more importantly, the values of the actors who constitute the movement. In many cities of the global South right-wing fundamentalist groups are very effective at mobilizing their members to engage in public displays of opposition and, sometimes, even hate-speech. Participation by the poor and marginalized citizens in social movements or processes can have a profoundly empowering psychic effect, as we know from the works and examples of Steven Biko, Paulo Freire, Mahatma Gandhi, Subcomandante Marcos, Frantz Fanon, Malcolm X, among others. However, this is contingent on the democratic culture of such organizations and the space for self-realization through experimentation and performative play. Ostensibly progressive agendas do not automatically translate into progressive interpersonal relations between activists; nor do they translate into self-realization as part and parcel of the larger social change desired by the movement. What I have in mind here is a form of politics sensitive to issues of interiority (psychic health) as well as exteriority.[26] This culturally attuned understanding of political agency is a vital part of redefining progressive political agency in our times. Surely our research of these movements needs to be as attuned to the political strategies and ideas as well as to the politics of self-realization. This is particularly important in the next domain of political practice.

Domain four: grassroots development practice

So long as we confine our conception of the political to activity that is openly declared we are driven to conclude that subordinate groups essentially lack a political life, or that what political life they do have is restricted to those exceptional moments of popular explosion. To do so is to miss the immense political terrain that lies between quiescence and revolt, and that, for better or worse, is the political environment of the subject classes. It is to focus on the visible coastline of politics and miss the continent that lies beyond.[27]

The public heroics of social movements are usually what grab our attention when we think about political agency in the city. However, as the work of James Scott suggests, the political terrain is much broader and more variegated than this. I am particularly interested in drawing attention to the everyday spaces and practices of grassroots development projects and their institutional frameworks. The politics of development practice unfolds at the neighbourhood scale (and beyond), where autonomous and state-dependent projects are undertaken to improve the quality of life and livelihoods, to protect against the vicissitudes of crime, violence and other shocks, and to deliberate future trajectories for the community in relation to other communities and the larger regional economic-ecological system.

In development studies there is a vast literature on the institutional dimensions of community-based development processes, with particular reference to anti-poverty programmes, which are most urgent for the urban poor.[28] In a similar sense, one could categorize shopfloor struggles to improve the quality of work and establish workplace democracy in this category. Both types of social practice involve the establishment of practical rules and norms that can regularize interactions between powerful interests (e.g. government departments with bundles of resources for specific programmes) and the various categories of poor citizens in terms of effective ways of meeting the minimum standards of 'human dignity' as espoused in national policies. In addition to clarifying norms and standards, grassroots development practice also involves the active construction of systematic projects to address a variety of consumption, productive, information and political needs. For example, savings associations, community gardens, neighbourhood watches, public art clubs, soup kitchens, shelters for the abused, community crèches, drama societies, religious clubs, sports organizations, primary health-care circles, and so on.

It is vital to appreciate the *experiential* importance of participation in community-based associations aimed at improving the quality of life of oneself and fellow residents. The recent work of Arjun Appadurai on slum-dweller associations in Mumbai argues for the importance of taking seriously 'the capacity to aspire' in thinking about this issue. Appadurai develops a layered argument that development, and especially its imagining, is deeply embedded in local cultures that people draw on to function in a day-to-day sense. Some of these cultural resources will be consistent with dominant societal values and norms that reproduce the acceptability of perverse inequalities. Other cultural resources may hold the germ of critique, of thinking about alternative social configurations that can lead to an improvement in quality of life and sense of self. The challenge is to use the future-shaping essence of development practice to expand 'the cultural map of aspirations' and in the process expand social citizenship and especially voice.[29] It is inconceivable that such political faculties can be cultivated outside an associational context. The argument can be extended. Social learning that arises from development projects can socialize uninformed and unrecognized citizens into democratic values such as accountability, transparency, (agonistic) deliberation, inclusivity, review and majority decision-making. In this sense, it prefigures the democratic rules of the larger political game that unfold in representative arenas. In other words, the experience of organizational democracy in development projects can concretize the meanings of democratic citizenship.

Furthermore, participation in development projects also enables people to see the bits and pieces of the state and how they function in contradictory ways at different scales. For example, those projects which benefit from, for instance, dedicated poverty funds, learn that the social development objectives of a national department may be very different to the social development initiatives of local government. In the larger political game, strategic political positioning and action depend on a differentiated understanding of the state and the contingent opportunities for alliances, when appropriate.[30] As long as organizations of the poor fail to capitalize on the always contingent contradictions between various arms of the state, they are unlikely to move their agendas forward, let alone recalibrate the priorities of the government.

Lastly, grassroots projects can be invaluable sites of experimentation with alternative ways of doing development. State bureaucracies tend to be rigid, hierarchical and conformist institutions. Little room is left for creativity, learning and innovation, despite incessant change management efforts.[31] In part, this is attributable to the organizational logic of large rule-bound and driven institutions. In part, it is a function of the need for political control and oversight over the functioning of government. The literature on organizational change and learning in the public sector suggests that these tendencies can only be mitigated by powerful external pressures that either show up the failures of government or provide compelling alternatives that allow new discourses to come into play.[32] On rare but very important occasions, grassroots initiatives can demonstrate alternative approaches to development that can be absorbed by the state and in theory lead to more equitable outcomes. A case in point is the influence of the South African Homeless People's Federation on the Department of Housing in South Africa and the government's subsequent adoption of the 'people's housing process' policy.[33]

These three instances make it clearer why grassroots development associations are such an important aspect of the larger political

canvas in the city. However, it would be misleading to suggest that
it is easy to achieve these impacts because of the dangers associated with this category of organization. Many of these grassroots
organizations operate in an apolitical fashion and tend to reproduce
welfarist models of social change. Such an approach deflects attention from the structural underpinning of maldistribution of public
resources. These organizations are also prone to co-option because
of financial dependency issues. This is less likely to be a problem
in cases where development projects also incorporate membership
fees/savings in the organizational methodology, but that is rare. One
insidious problem is the potential of development projects to dissipate
pent-up anger and militancy – the fuel of 'spontaneous' combustion
that is so essential for direct action.

In terms of the overall conceptual model proposed here, it is
important to review grassroots development practice in relation to
neo-corporatist forums and the departmental programmes carried out
by municipal government. Due to the inherently tame and consensual
style of politics that one finds in this sphere, it can be anticipated
that umbrella organizations of this grassroots type are likely to
participate in multi-stakeholder deliberative forums ostensibly to
represent 'the community' voice. This makes such organizations of
strategic importance to social movements that may prefer to stand
outside the discursive ambit of deliberative forums. On many issues,
informal alliances with these organizations will complement public
actions to good effect. On other issues, social movements may wish
to back their positions and agendas in these forums through the
media and other forms of projection and agitation in the public
domain. On every issue of note in the city, symbolic politics will
be key, and symbolism thrives on waves of compelling and widely
shared messages. With this point it is appropriate to move on to
a discussion of domain five of political practice: symbolic politics
through discursive action.

Domain five: symbolic politics

[P]ower is both embedded in and effectuated through a crucial
combination of knowledge and language, or what is called discourse. Discourse in this sense is the complex mixture of ideas and
expressions through which individuals both perceive and in turn

try to explain social reality. Discourse therefore also defines the parameters and criteria people use to ascertain and calculate the *potential courses of action* and to choose particular courses of action in specific circumstances. It is thus the primary ... medium of both understanding and action.[34]

Paradoxically, the symbolic or discursive domain is the most under-studied and undertheorized compared to the previous four domains of practice, because, as Michel Foucault suggests, we are surrounded and enrolled by discursive power all the time. It is the ground we move on, the air we breathe, because we cannot step outside of it if we are to make a (conscious or unconscious) decision about our next move. Discourses provide a lens on the world, our everyday spaces and ourselves. They constitute the everyday and specialist knowledge we draw on to make sense of larger systems of power that shape thought and behaviour through regulation of bodily practices. Put differently, we internalize discourses about the issues it is appropriate to consider, what to think about (or believe of) such issues, and how to act in ways consistent with what we believe, and of course to rationalize it if we do not manage to do so. All of this comes to us as unquestionable truths and that is the core of the power of discourse. It renders certain historically and politically constructed assumptions as self-evident and obvious, beyond the remit of questioning or reversal. For discursive power to work its magic, it must insinuate itself culturally – that is, be embedded in our daily sensibilities and practices, which are culturally specific and contingent. Here I am applying a notion of culture as

> the historical transmission of a learned repertory of embodied human practices expressed in symbolic codes through which individuals and social groups develop and perpetuate a way of life. It is a set of signify-ing activities shaped by and infused with relations of power. Culture implies not only language, values, beliefs, and mores, but material objects and processes organized in time–space locations. Culture is therefore a complex social ecology of object, subject, and intersubjective relations.[35]

For my purposes in this chapter, I want to draw attention to the political potency of discourses about the *identity of the city* and the policy imperatives that flow from it. In a recent article, Jenny

Robinson highlights the problematic obsession of many local government managers in the global South with becoming 'world class' and 'globally competitive'.[36] The discourse on the imperative of becoming world class or globally competitive leads inexorably to policy commitments to maintain levels of infrastructure that are deemed world class and favourable to attracting foreign investors. If such high-cost and high-maintanance infrastructures are not sufficiently *in place*, literally, then of course investment strategies need to be devised to ensure that sufficient resources are mobilized to make such 'essential' investments possible.[37] If this means that fewer resources are available for investing in infrastructure-poor areas, especially in times of economic slowdown, then this is a rational sacrifice for the longer term good of the city. In this context, neo-corporatist forums then become important sites of reproducing and legitimating such discourses to the point of expunging oppositional ones, or at least casting such perspectives as 'out of touch with reality'. Crucially, municipal discourses such as these are reinforced by national discourses as expressed through the macroeconomic commitments of the government and the industrial strategy that prioritizes investment in high-tech sectors that will enable emerging developing economies to 'compete' globally, irrespective of whether the educational base exists for the realization of such an economic trajectory. If one reflects on the underlying economic rationale of the CDS policy discourses, it is apparent how they can be manipulated to legitimate the economic preoccupation of urban elites to do whatever it takes to become 'competitive' and 'world class', even if it involves decisions that will cause the poor to suffer even more hardship in the short term. In the rationality of such policy discourses, short-term suffering is a necessary evil in order first to grow the economy, which will generate the resources eventually to attend more effectively to the needs of the poor.

If cities in the global South are to become spaces of greater possibility for radical democracy and distributive justice, this domain of political practice will have to be taken much more seriously. Symbolic contestation through the deconstruction and reconstruction of dominant discourses is a prerequisite for achieving impact in terms of political strategies in all four of the other domains discussed earlier.

Symbolic politics functions through cultural resignification and therefore implies more creative practices which target the media, especially radio and popular newspapers; public spaces in the city, especially streetscapes and squares invested with symbolic meaning; and spaces of collective consumption, such as schools, clinics, libraries. Symbolic contestation clears the ground to ask fundamental questions about given governmental discourses, such as: What are the underlying rationalities of this discourse? What conditions make it possible for this discourse to pass as given and valid? What are the goals of the discourse? How can the elements of the discourse be challenged and rearranged to turn the discourse on itself and make new meanings and imaginings possible which can be pursued through direct action or development practice or municipal policy? More presciently, to return to my earlier concern about the identity of the city, a discursive sensitivity makes it possible to recast questions such as these: Who is the city for? Whose identities and cultures are embodied by representations of the city? How can the futures of the city be re-imagined to reflect a radical openess as opposed to the conventional approach whereby there is only one alternative?[38]

Interfaces

The drawback of any conceptual model is that it superimposes a false sense of structure on complex and fluid social realities. The conceptual model of urban politics developed here is no exception. A lot of dynamics leak from the model to smudge the artificial boundaries between urban spaces and associated political practices. As Arjun Appadurai reminds us, cultural identities and practices are constitutively porous, relational and marked by dissensus within some aspiration for consensus. For these reasons, it is important to foreground the numerous spaces between different types of political practice. I will consider one striking example that is theorized in the evocative work of Asef Bayat on what he categorizes as 'the encroachment of the ordinary'.

Asef Bayat, in the tradition of James Scott, seeks to capture political agency in a zone in between what I would label direct action and development practice.[39] Bayat studies the everyday practices of survival and circumvention, undertaken at the expense of the elite, that the ultra poor engage in to carve out spaces to dwell, move around and earn an income in the city where their very presence is deemed illegitimate and illegal. It is a nuanced and layered argument which is best summarized by the author:

> The notion of 'quiet encroachment' describes the silent, protracted and pervasive advancement of ordinary people on those who are propertied and powerful in a quest for survival and improvement of their lives. It is characterized by quiet, largely atomized and prolonged mobilization with episodic collective action – open and fleeting struggles without clear leadership, ideology or structured organization. While quiet encroachment is basically a 'non-movement', it is distinct from survival strategies or 'everyday resistance'. First, the struggles and gains of people at the grassroots are not made at the expense of fellow poor or themselves, but of the state, the rich and the general public. For example, in order to light their shelters, the urban poor tap electricity not from their neighbours, but from the municipality power poles; to raise their living standard they do not prevent their children from attending school and send them to work, but rather they squeeze the hours of their own formal job in order to work a second job in the informal sector. In addition, these struggles should not be seen as necessarily defensive, merely in the realm of 'resistance', but as cumulatively encroaching, meaning that the actors tend to expand their space by winning new positions to move on to. This kind of quiet activism challenges fundamental aspects of state prerogatives, including the meaning of 'order' and control of public space. But the most immediate consequence is the redistribution of social goods via the (unlawful and direct) acquisition of: collective consumption (land, shelter, piped water, electricity); public space (streets, intersections, parking areas); and opportunities (favourable business conditions, locations and labels).[40]

This provocative conception clearly has resonance and relevance across the global South if one considers the slum growth trends outlined in Chapter 2 and the evocative overviews by Mike Davis (*Planet of Slums*) and Robert Neuwirth (*A Billion Squatters*). Yet it would be incorrect to locate it as either direct action or politics of development practice. It occupies a zone in between but is also highly amenable for deployment in creative politics of discursive contestation about who the city is for, even if not by the protagonists of quiet encroachment themselves. This example will have to suffice to stress the point that the model can only be seen as a heuristic device to explore discrete domains of political practice and their hybrid interfaces. Now for some comments on the final elements of the model depicted in Figure 5.1: political and public spheres.

Public sphere + political sphere = vibrant democracy?

In terms of the conceptual model, elected politicians carry out their function primarily in two domains of political practice: the representative sphere and neo-corporatist forums. And together these two constitute the formal 'political sphere' in the city, anchored in the deliberations of the municipal council chamber. In the political sphere the governmental priorities of the city are defined, contested and reviewed through highly structured procedural mechanisms of deliberation. Both the content and the systems of deliberation have a structuring effect on what is defined as legitimately part of the political sphere and what is not. As I have already argued, discursive power and its underlying knowledges are the grids that define the horizon of political imagination and intervention. This political horizon is mediated via the media and legitimating knowledge institutions such as universities, technical colleges, think-tanks and opinion-poll survey companies that reflect back to society curves of opinion and attitudes with a gloss of scientificity. In the absence of dissent and conflict, the political sphere can easily dominate and structure the broader public sphere where state and civil society engagements are mediated. In other words, top-down political practices can eclipse bottom-up processes that emanate from civil society, effectively asphyxiating democratic citizenship.

For this reason, it is vital to stimulate and animate a vibrant public sphere. In the traditional Habermasian sense, the public sphere 'is a space which mediates between society and the state where the public organizes itself and in which "public opinion" is formed'.[41] In this sphere, citizens engage discursively and rationally in public reasoning to arrive at the greatest public interest on a given issue. My theoretical starting points at the beginning of the chapter lead me away from the rational deliberative model of Habermas in order to promote a conception of the public sphere more favourable to the possibility and hegemony of radical democracy. This refers to 'a radical pluralistic public sphere of contestive identities, moralities, and discourses. It endorses a politics of diverse social, cultural and political movements organized around the values of cultural recognition, direct democracy, and performative resistance.[42] This conception is premissed on the insight of Chantal Mouffe that we can never fully reconcile the tensions between equality (maximization of egalitarian spaces of differences) and liberty (maximization of democratic rights), but instead deploy the tension to animate agonistic contestation within the ambit of universal human rights.[43] The tension produces agonistic pluralism in the polity. In summary, the argument here is simply for a recognition that at the nexus of the present (everyday transgressions in combination with an agonistic public-political sphere), the past (memory) and the future (open-ended), we are perched on the edge of a politics of potentiality – that is, a transgressive politics of radical democracy and distributive justice.

Conclusion

By crossing the limits of possibility one encounters transgression. The perverse persistence of brutal inequality in cities of the South requires a politics of transgression that valorizes agonistic engagement in a radical democratic public sphere. An ethic of transgression is a prerequisite for political action that will shift the 'frontier of the possible', following the injunction of Ben Okri. In this chapter I have attempted to clarify a conceptual model of urban politics that can serve two functions. On the one hand, it can stimulate a stronger *relational* perspective of urban political practices across a plurality of action spaces – formal and informal, symbolic and concrete, collaborative and contestationary – with a sensibility of agonistic pluralism. Too much of the current scholarship on urban development is fragmented and partial, undermining our ability to get a handle on what is going on and how the status quo is maintained and bolted in place. This aspect of the model is about incitement to more comprehensive analytical accounts of political practices in the city – that is, the fullness of political identities in variegated time-spaces of the city.

On the other hand, I have also sought to demonstrate that a radical democratic practice in the city is multidimensional and constitutively open-ended. If one considers the multiplicity of domains of political practice alongside the subjective imperative of identity politics, it is clear that progressive politics cannot be imagined *a priori*, or in simple good/bad terms. A progressive agenda is by definition a complex lattice of numerous transgressive practices that span from psychic interiors to the monumental spaces that symbolically 'embody' the city for its citizens and the world at large. In between there are an infinite series of strategic and tactical manoeuvres that can be deployed to remake political identities, boundaries and horizons. It is only at the coalface of practice and resistance that the tactical coordinates can be defined and used as a resource to construct focused political communities in difference and solidarity. Such an appreciation allows for the natural coming together of an unflinching critique of the workings of dominating power, especially during our neoliberal times, and reverence for the complexity and indeterminacy of political practice. For me, echoing James Holston, this constitutes the challenge, pleasure and joy of insurgent citizenship for the city yet to come.[44] The next chapter takes a detour via 'the insurgent' to balance out the formalistic policy argument that follows.

6

Informal everyday urbanism

At the core of the mainstream view on cities, and slums, in the developing world is a topos that locates these places on a continuum from nascent/informal to developed/post-industrial, with the latter representing the apex of human achievement in city building. This is explicitly captured in the *Guide to City Development Strategies*, which proposes a 'stylised urban development trajectory', with an economic continuum from informal economy to high-tech, high-design amenity services.[1] Implicit in this kind of perspective is a desire progressively to move the chaotic, malfunctioning city of informality towards a situation of order, comprehension and optimal functioning, with the humanist intent of course that everyone who lives in the city should enjoy a reasonable and dignified quality of life. On the back of this desire for steady improvement is a belief in the power of (rational) planning and deliberation to agree on the necessary actions/interventions to improve the quality of life of, especially, the urban poor and vulnerable, as we saw in Chapter 4. In this mindset it is broadly accepted, even if not always practised, that to get this right the intended beneficiaries must be actively involved and drive the process. This narrative tends to function on the basis of an assumption that modern, gleaming, skyscraper-filled cities, with adequate networked infrastructures in place to support them, is the only and ineluctable way into the urban future.

This is a dangerous policy mindset because it reinforces and legiti-
mizes a form of governmentality – disciplinary, control and regulatory
actions – that makes it acceptable to intervene recklessly in the lives
and livelihoods of millions of poor people without appreciating the
delicate networks and strategies these denizens rely on to survive the
city in the domain of the informal. Thus, the purpose of this chapter
is to foreground the practices, dynamics, potentialities that reside
beyond the state's reach and understanding, but are fundamental to
the 'multiplex' identities of the territories subjected to various forms of
urban development.[2] In the first section I argue that it is as plausible
to build a conceptual model of the city from the perspective of the
slum as it is from the perspective of the formal, concrete-and-steel city,
as is normally done. This attempt at a conceptual inversion is used as
a prelude to explore the city from the bottom up, or rather through
the eyes of the majority of poor denizens who appropriate the city for
their own ends. The examples range from Asef Bayat's paradigmatic
work on the 'encroachment of the ordinary', to an exploration of the
mobilization logics or counter-governmentalities of the Shack/Slum
Dwellers International, to imaginative re-representation of slums in
Caracas, and then to promising examples where these logistics, along
with an interest in public culture, are the resources of reformulation
of the nature and potentialities of the urban in the South. The central
theme of this chapter, and of the book, is that a deeper appreciation
of cultural identities and dynamics that play out in the lived realities
of daily life and symbolic manifestations is a prerequisite for more
appropriate urban transformations.

Conceptual inversion

In a recent book by Nigel Coates, *Guide to Ecstacity*, the modernist urban imaginary is fundamentally challenged and supplanted
by the imaginative invention of an alternative conceptual map and
vocabulary to try to define what alternative urbanisms may feel, taste,
sound, look and smell like.[3] Given the fresh and subversive novelty
of this affective imaginary, a few definitional fragments from the
book are quoted here:

> [I]n Ecstacity ... we should rise to the challenge of how locality, iden-
> tity, freedom, diversity and security can be addressed together.

Ecstacity models a world that emphasizes local identity rather than some corporate ideology. Its particularity is in its variety, not its uniformity. As if in a Borgesian multidimensional space, it reinstates the empathy between the imagination and the everyday. It sets out to unite and respect the multiplicity of the world we live in rather than erect the sort of barriers that exacerbate misunderstanding.

Furthermore,

Ecstacity is about ideas, relations and blended conditions. Its premise is that, first and foremost, the city should be a place of experience before the formal stylistic or functional qualities of buildings [or dwellings]. In it, architecture – or its own broad version of it – is a vehicle for a looser and more open framework that stimulates the space in each of us … it sets out the city as if a dynamic paradigm for each of its multi-various inhabitants, every one of whom can act as both stimulator and respondent.

Granted, the architecturally driven vision of Coates can be seen as a mere distraction by an eloquent fantasist who takes energy and focus away from the pressing problem of slums and their attendant poverty. However, my reading is that our present thinking about meeting the challenges of slums is profoundly impoverished precisely because we locate these places with their teeming complexities in a black box devoid of complex agency and determinacy, which is nonetheless unconsciously ascribed to parts of the modern city that are considered developed or settled. Thus Coates's argument can be interpreted as an extension of a long tradition of urban anthropology and sociology which seeks to ascribe and analyse patterns of agency among all city dwellers, whether in slums or not.[4] It is of course the implications of such literature that have given rise to the shift in urban development policy discourses away from 'needs' and 'absences', to focus instead on the 'assets' and 'capabilities' of urban dwellers; a move that has spawned the burgeoning literature on urban livelihoods.[5] There is no doubt that this seam of research and theorizing has greatly improved the capacity of local governments, NGOs and other urban development agencies to understand better the opportunities for support and enhancement of local practices in slums.

However, my argument here attempts to go somewhat deeper. In my reading, unless we are able to re-imagine fundamentally the nature of the urban and the multiple potentialities of the city, by virtue of the culturally sutured practices of the diverse people who live there, we will not be able to move beyond essentially technocratic conceptualizations of city improvement. The question that I am groping with is this: why can we not see slums as *constitutive* of the city as are, say, the suburbs, or the central business districts, or the luminous commercial retail spaces that serve to anchor middle-class existences in the postmodern city? Given that in most cities in the global South the majority of citizens live in slums, is it not time to rethink our epistemic categories and redefine the city through the practices of the slum, and other areas, in order to come to terms with 'the complexity of human nature, and how it wobbles constantly between pragmatism and significance, between pleasure seeking and survival.'[6] And, of course, to explore how the complexity of human nature is expressed in the creation, experience and remaking of space as an incessant series of manoeuvres to make life worthwhile and meaningful, even if the desire that dominates is to find a job, or anything that will generate cash, or a corrugated sheet of metal to fortify a leaking wall of a shack, or enough to buy a cold beer at the local drinking hole where the woman of your dreams works as a cleaner...

It is in this sense that I think the *Ecstacity* provocations of Coates are apt. We have to step back, climb outside our mental cages and completely rethink the ways in which we talk about, imagine and seek to impact on life and desires in slums. This means being able to locate slums within a larger matrix of urbanism which contextualizes not the slums alone, but the very possibility of the suburb, or the high-consumption gay spaces in the city, or sites of leisure and retail concentrated in shopping malls that stand as sentinels at the edges of sprawled cities. From this angle, we are forced to question the adequacy of our concepts, policy frameworks and, of course, good intentions.

Clearly, a fuller, rounded and dense matrix of urbanism can only be approached and grasped through a strong cultural perspective. As intimated before, it is precisely such a perspective that I find singularly missing, or, rather, thin in the mainstream accounts of the city, and especially the dynamics of slums. Instead, what is typically projected is a litany of statistics to capture (physical and social)

infrastructural and economic absences, stylized accounts of livelihood patterns to give one a sense of everyday economies and levels
of dependency on mutual support and/or state investments, and
possibly broad brush-strokes on levels of associational involvement,
especially in organizations focused on livelihood improvement. These
informational coordinates are, of course, important and relevant, but
they typically reveal a lot less than they conceal. Without a nuanced
exploration of social and psychic dynamics in poor areas, our understanding of these communities and the urban system within which
they are embedded will remain inadequate for the realization of the
imagination and politics that can lead to truly audacious interventions.
Overleaf, towards the end of the chapter, I return to these themes by
exploring examples where popular culture and literary registers offer
far more compelling representations of everyday life in slums.

One of the frustrating aspects of urban development is the fact
that it is relatively easy to identify the causal drivers of the multi-
tude of problems that characterize most cities in the global South.
However, it does not follow that solutions to these problems are
straightforward to pinpoint and pursue. As I suggested at the outset,
this disjuncture compels one to pursue a transformation agenda that
is systemic and systematic – that is, invariably incremental – but
also radical in that it seeks over time to shift the underlying causal
factors that reproduce urban injustice. It is difficult to maintain this
fine balance because the rationalities and institutional intensities
of mainstream urban management can completely overwhelm and
swamp critical actors in the state and in civil society. This is where
insurgent practices come into the frame. Insurgent practices take on
various forms but essentially reflect autonomous efforts on the part
of urban citizens in various kinds of associational configurations to
carve our a space for their interests and desires despite regulatory
or symbolic prescriptions of the state. I now turn to the most useful
conceptual attempt to capture and theorize such insurgencies.

Insurgent urbanism: encroachment of the ordinary

The big controversy over the approach of the Millennium Development Goals (MDGs) to the issue of shelter is of course the pathetic
target of lifting 100 million slum dwellers out of poverty by 2015.

What this target says is that if all the actors in the world who deal with urban development put their heads together and prioritize the eradication of slum living conditions, then 90 percent (900 million) of slum dwellers worldwide will have to accept that they are not part of this deal; their lives will not be touched by this extraordinary global effort. Let us put the moral problems of this form of ultra-conservative targeting to one side; let us also ignore the stacks of academic reviews piling up predicting a massive failure to achieve the MDG targets, given the trends since 2000 when the targets were agreed upon. Instead, let us assume the target will be met. What does it mean for the everyday reality of the world's urban population, largely confined to unhealthy, precarious and overcrowded condi-tions? Basically, it means that people will continue to live in the ways they live today: by their wits, relentlessly inventive and within powerful networks of support and symbiotic dependence.

However, inside urban development policy discourses that seek to spell out the solutions to problems, there is very little room for a deep consideration or appreciation of the agency, skill, endurance and effort that go into the survival and consolidation strategies of the urban poor. The 'livelihoods' literature has stepped into this breach and can offer great insights. However, it very easily slips into a 'toolbox' discourse that helps urban planners or developers to understand the livelihood strategies of the poor so as to better connect them to micro-finance, or institutional support, and thereby enlarge their 'stocks of social capital'. There is a place for this form of engagement with the survival practices of the poor, but it cannot substitute for a serious engagement with the 'quiet encroachment practices' of thousands, and sometimes millions, of individual actions outside of modern institutions. In the previous chapter I quoted Asef Bayat at some length to reflect his conceptualization of this idea of rich, below-the-radar sets of small actions to gain a little piece of pavement, or a few square foot of floor space, or illegally tapped kilowatts from a government-owned power line, or enough invisibility to duplicate copyrighted goods for sale at informal markets; all actions carried out by the 'necessity to survive and live a dignified life'.[7] Since most slum dwellers and other marginal people in urban areas are essentially left to fend for themselves without the prospect of state

support or decent work, by sheer dint of necessity people make do
and invent an endless series of permutations of informalized work,
service provision, occupation, places for bodily relief and passion.
Mostly these activities take on the form of modest, surreptitious
and atomized actions to carve out a little foothold to secure sustenance for just another day. From time to time they can spill over
into more collective expressions of demand, but according to Bayat
the aim is usually to defend illegally gotten gains in the city. Conceptually, Asef Bayat suggests, we need to understand two primary
aims that are embedded in these inevitable and incessant dynamics
of encroachment in contemporary cities in the South:

> The first [aim] is the redistribution of social goods and opportuni-
> ties in the form of the (unlawful and direct) acquisition of collective
> consumption (land, shelter, piped water, electricity, roads), public space
> (street sidewalks, intersections, street parking places), opportunities
> (favourable business conditions, locations, and labels), and other life
> changes essential for survival and a minimal standard of living.
>
> The other goal is attaining *autonomy*, both cultural and political,
> from the regulations, institutions, and discipline imposed by the state.
> The disenfranchised express a deep desire to live an informal life,
> to run their own affairs without involving the authorities or other
> modern formal institutions. This is not to suggest that tradition guides
> their lives, but rather to insist that modern institutions, in one sense,
> reproduce people's traditional relations as solutions to the problems
> that these institutions engender. In many informal communities in
> Third World cities, people rely on their own local and traditional norms
> during their daily activities, whether it be establishing contracts (e.g.
> marriage), organizing their locality, or resolving local disputes. In a way,
> they are compelled to exert control over their working lives, regulating
> their time and coordinating their space ... autonomy and integration in
> the view of both the poor and the state are far from straightforward.
> They are the subject of contradictory processes, constant redefinition,
> and intense negotiation. Informality is not an essential preference of
> the urban poor; it serves primarily as an alternative to the constraints
> of formal structures.[8]

Clearly, for as long as the contemporary capitalist system persists,
exacting particular forms of territorial management – uneven and
highly exclusionary – it is likely that it will serve the interest of the
majority of the poor better to retain their autonomy and cannibalize

formal systems and resources where they can; and to bend parts of the city to their will by defending and consolidating the micro-gains they succeed in making by simply surviving the viciousness of the city's economic reproduction. Significant for me is the sheer scale and density of these practices across most of the South because of the similarity in economic and governmental conditions, which leave little room for the rights of the disenfranchised to be recognized and realized. Despite the obvious prevalence and scale of these actions, it is telling that the bulk of urban scholarship, and of course policy discourse, simply bypasses these dynamics and rather creates urban spaces that correspond with the regulatory and developmental criteria of formalized modern systems of urban management.

Tenacious insurgent activism: Shack/Slum Dwellers International[9]

If Asef Bayat's work draws attention to the logic of atomized encroachment on the formal city, the next example draws attention to a category of urban actors who use their marginality as a source of active mobilization to extract concessions and services from the state, but, crucially, on their own terms. The most coherent, well-connected and articulate of the various slum associations in the world is undoubtedly Shack/Slum Dwellers International (SDI). As a network they have been incredibly effective and influential in shaping shelter and tenure policies of international development agencies over the past few years, as discussed in Chapter 4. In this section, I want to home in on their unique ideology and mobilization practice because it points to one way of turning marginality and autonomy into an institutional expression that can create an effective interface with the state without giving up entirely the few sources of power available to the urban poor. Given the great diversity of various affiliated federations of the SDI, I will use the one I am most familiar with, the South African Homeless People's Federation (SAHPF), to explore this theme.

The institutional architecture of the SAHPF is deliberatively designed to support an unambiguously people-led, people-centred and people-controlled development strategy, termed in academic literature as asset-based community development. This approach is about fostering transformative, self-reliant and self-replicable social development practices modelled around: asset mobilization; asset mapping; community-based problem solving; and 'progressive scaling' up of activities as outside external institutions are called upon to invest in community-devised and locally driven development initiatives. Key practices or rituals to give effect to this strategy include: enumeration and mapping, surveying, house modelling and savings schemes establishment, exchange visits between settlements and internationally, precedent setting and claim-making.

In contrast to mainstream claim-making practices, the HPA's strategy in its engagement with the state is underpinned by the belief that official programmes 'need to be redesigned and redeveloped by the poor' so that they 'work for them', followed by negotiation with the state to obtain support for the implementation of their 'solution'.[10] The solutions championed aim to strengthen long-term capacity- and capability-building through three linked change processes: asset-building (mobilizing social capital through federating, networking and exchanges, savings and loan activities); developing a knowledge of community priorities and needs and how best to meet them, and accumulating and mobilizing resources to test the efficacy and sustainability of the solution (via enumeration, community planning and house design exercises, supported by exchange visits); and engaging the state to support the solutions engineered by the poor, without strangling the 'life out of their organizations'.[11]

A key outcome of these processes of capacity–capability enhancement is for the poor to lead by example, wherein communities pioneer and develop their own solution and demonstrate its practical viability – precedent-setting – before engaging the state in an effort to transform official programmes. Of significance in this approach is not pitting the solution proposed by the poor against the state programme, or lobbying directly for policy change, but rather the seeking of 'shifts' in the *institutional arrangements* which determine the way policy translates into action. The 'attendant shifts in the institutional framework, if they are of some magnitude, will be bound to have a direct impact on policy'.[12] Joel Bolnick, director of SDI, captured the spirit of this form of engagement most eloquently: 'Don't confront authority head on. Instead of storming the citadel, infiltrate it.... Play judo with the state – use its own weight to roll it over.'[13]

Clearly, the modalities of state engagement are extremely sophisticated. It involves straddling diverse spatial scales and territorial–
administrative jurisdictions; criss-crossing the political and official
divide; deal-making with progressive and conservative political parties;
and playing off one level of government against another (among
others). This strategic practice arises from and is reinforced by multi-
scalar organization-building interventions (local/regional/national/
international exchanges and affiliation to Shack/Slum Dwellers International[14]) whose roots are anchored in communities.

The 'federating' of community-based organizations at city, provincial and national scales is the first step. Once federations are
active, negotiation with government officials commences around
the priorities of the poor, and the solutions devised by them. Significant in SAHPF's multi-scalar practice are the contributions of
the international donor community. The flexibility of donor funding
facilitates innovation, which is needed to ensure effective utilization
of government funds.[15] Donor funding also creates the multinational
language and legitimacy for SAHPF interventions.

The superior track record of this unique community-based development approach is most visible in the SAHPF's widely celebrated
housing delivery strategy. While the state was finalizing its supply
side, state-facilitated and private-sector-driven housing programme (in
a forum that excluded the homeless poor and their organizations),
the SAHPF used a combination of uTshani Fund loans (their own
loan finance facility, capitalized at that stage by European donors)
and savings from collectives of poor people to build homes that
were larger, cheaper and of better quality than those delivered via
the state–developer partnership route. In other words, in a context
such as South Africa, where there was a state-driven public housing
programme, the SAHPF could outperform the state in terms of
process and outcome with far fewer resources. This is a significant
achievement by any measure.

The SAHPF model became increasingly attractive to government.
Following the promotion of the model as sustainable at the Habitat
II Conference in 1996, global donors[16] provided direct support for
the adoption of a housing approach based on self-help construction
through the formation of a People's Housing Partnership Trust within

the Department of Housing of the South African government in 1998. The purpose of the Trust was the 'institutional capacitation and empowerment at the provincial and local spheres of government and among NGOs to support the peoples' process'.[17]

In South Africa, poor people are placed on a waiting list, and when their turn comes they get the free transfer of a built house, with serviced land, usually no more than 32 square metres. Under the People's Housing Process provision of the government, introduced in May 1998, potential beneficiaries had to demonstrate participation in a savings scheme in order to access the capital subsidy allocated to the top structure of public housing. Considerable emphasis was placed by government on community or beneficiary contribution to the process of house construction through sweat equity. Thus the official people's housing process approach became ostensibly about people building their own houses utilizing subsidized materials, with government extending the necessary infrastructure.[18] The SAHPF and many progressive development practitioners claim the adoption of people's housing processes by the state as an important victory for those committed to people-centred development.

Mainstreaming into government policy an alternative, initially insurgent, survival practice is a noteworthy achievement. However, as our research demonstrates, this can come at a cost in terms of the effectiveness and radical edge of the movement. Today the SDI is a profoundly influential actor on the world stage of urban development policymaking but remains wedded to a radical, oppositional political ideology. For example, on their website they assert:

> The SDI affiliates have come together to give a voice to the poor in an arena of decision-making that has, in recent years, been confined to global organizations that champion neoliberal theories of development. As a counterpoint to these agencies, social movements (such as the women's and environmental movements) have emerged. They see themselves as opponents of centralized state power, backed by these global agencies – the United Nations, the International Monetary Fund and the World Bank.[19]

The reason they are able to hold seemingly contradictory positions – opposition and cooperation – is perceptively distilled by Mark Swilling:

BOX 6.1 Urban Think Tank: Caracas Case

A number of photographers, visual artists, architects and writers, as well as social and cultural scientists, came together to research the informal influences on the contemporary development of urban culture in Latin America, taking Caracas as an example. The results of the interdisciplinary field research provided the basis for a fascinating publication, *Informal City: Caracas Case*, a work that is of great relevance beyond Caracas and puts up for discussion a new form of informal urbanism. A central argument by the lead researchers/instigators/editors is the following:

> The approach we take in this book to understanding the 21st-century city offers an alternative to that of traditional planning, which has attempted to shape the city over the past centuries and has been rooted in European rationalism, notwithstanding resistance. Indeed, it has long been an article of faith among architects and planners that the Cartesian model is required in order to analyse the city, to the extent that no definition of the 'informal city' even exists.... The absence of zoning codes, and well-established private property rights and the existence of alternatively organized communities was seen as primitive and problematic. [However, the] planned city can neither eliminate nor subsume the informal qualities and practices of its inhabitants. The informal city persists; its inherent strengths resist and defeat efforts to impose order. The totally planned city is, therefore, a myth.... The present-day city calls for a profound reorientation in the manner in which we study it; we believe in working at the intersections of the individual and the collective, the real and the virtual in a multiplicity of parallel engagements.

The book and accompanying exhibitions are wonderfully illustrated with a melange of essays, photographs, diagrams, illustrative sampling, statistics and maps and were actively inserted into ongoing public debates and public processes.

The significance of the approach used by the SDI associated initiatives is that they have plaited together strands of developmental knowledge that are normally compartmentalized into separate types of developmental practice: the key role of micro-finance in development; grassroots community-organizing to build collective solidarities; technical innovations aimed at doing more with less; challenging existing inequalities at the political level; pragmatic autonomism within civil society; the specificity of the city and in particular the socio-cultural context of the urban poor as a field of organizational practice; and subordinating professional knowledge and roles to the organized chaos of community leadership. Unsurprisingly, as with any kind of synthesis, it makes everyone who has not seen the synthesis unhappy. The pragmatic autonomism will be criticized for being reformist because it 'lets the state off the hook'; the emphasis on continuous challenge and engagement will be criticized for being too political and confrontational thus putting potential concessions at risk; micro-finance combined with community organizing will be criticized by the micro-finance purists for being irresponsible; and traditional rights-based community organizers will see micro-finance as a waste of energy when the real task should be to put pressure on states to inject more development finance. Above all else, synthesis often makes the story too complex to tell in short and simple enough ways for academics, government officials, the media, development specialists and most social activists to understand. It works in communities because this complexity is an everyday reality.[20]

I will conclude this section on this note because it demonstrates clearly the central point of this chapter: namely, in both the atomized and organized survival practices of the poor, most of the lessons and knowledge gained in engaging with the complexity of urban areas are already decipherable, but the conventional assumptions and policy models are not tuned in. Box 6.1 describes a fascinating effort to take the constitutive nature of urban informality as a starting point for radically rethinking the city from the vantage point of Caracas.[21] This vital work, which I do not have the space here to explore more fully, provides an important example of one alternative way to respond to the insurgent energies that invariably arise from the cauldrons of informality across the South.

Popular culture and the negotiation of everyday violence

The literature is clear that urban violence is often endemic in many cities of South. One of the more extreme examples is Brazil, where violence is indeed a dominant factor in everyday life, particularly in the enclave neighbourhoods where the poor are concentrated – the *favelas*. A consequence of this dominance is the normalization of violence as routine in resolving conflict or relating to others. The literature suggests that this is particularly common in post-conflict societies such as Colombia,[22] Nicaragua,[23] South Africa,[24] Jamaica,[25] among many others.[26] Drug trafficking finds an easy setting in these societies because it requires and produces violence. Almost all dimensions of the drug trade involve violence; for example, gang warfare that flares to control markets and turf, attacks on addicts in waves of social cleansing (especially in Brazil), and the incessant quarrels and gendered interpersonal violence in the home.[27]

Structural violence, associated in particular with drug economies, gave rise to particular spatial configurations in *favelas* which constrict and direct the movement of ordinary people. Urban planner/ethnographer Marcelo Lopez de Sousa, in *Culture Is Our Weapon*, provides an insightful picture of this spatiality:

> *favela*-based retail drug trafficking combines a strong hierarchy at the scale of the *favela*, with a decentralised, network-based organisation at the *comandos* scale. In each shanty town, this hierarchy comprises (in descending order): the *dono do morro* ('owner of the hill'), *gerentes* ('managers', those who control the selling places), *soldados* ('soldiers', security staff), *vapores* ('vapours', street sellers) and *aviões* ('aeroplanes', go-between sellers). Each drug trafficking crew or *quadrilha* has its own territory of one or more *favelas*, and while dealers who belong to the same *comando* usually respect each other's territories, bandits belonging to rival *comandos* often try to take possession of enemy territories. This results in turf wars over several days or even weeks, usually involving several drug trafficking crews belonging to the same *comando* in the spirit of mutual help. The protection of business as well as other, more symbolic aspects such as demonstrations of power and virility … has contributed not only to an increasing use of violence among criminal crews, but also to an increasing atmosphere of tyranny for *favela* inhabitants.[28]

The evocative accounts by former *traficantes* (drug traffickers) captures how a willingness and capacity for violence are key to moving up the rungs of the drug gangs, in terms of both status and space. The net effect of the violence is staggering: 'between 1948 and 1999, an estimated 13 000 people were killed in the Israeli–Palestinian conflict. Between 1979 and 2000, more than 48 000 died from firearm related injuries in the city of Rio.'[29] In other words, young black kids in Rio's *favelas* grow up in a war zone, possibly with worse psycho-social impacts because no one regards it as a time of war.[30] However, amidst this bleak outlook, dynamic counterpoints have also emerged to respond to these trends, but crucially using a popular-cultural hook.

Musical genres such as hip-hop and reggae, fused with indigenous genres such as *forró*, *frevo*, *samba*, *bossa nova*, Brazilian rock, among others, have been central to the fermentation of a popular source of critique and alternative practices to the violent gang cultures that dominate everyday life in *favelas*. For example, Racionais MCs, the enormously popular hip-hop group from São Paulo, rap almost exclusively about their position of marginality and the ways in which the dominant, racist system reproduces that marginality.[31] Another equally influential and critical voice is MV Bill from Rio de Janeiro, who more clearly takes on the position of 'organic intellectual' from the *favela* who aims to 'speak truth to power' about the double standards of mainstream assumptions in Brazilian society:

> [W]hat you have to understand about this society is that questions of violence and crime are not just about guns and drugs. In Brazil, the only people who go to prison are those who steal a little. Those who steal a lot go free. Putting people in sub-human conditions in the *favelas*? When I show it I'm criticised but that's a form of violence. In Rio, there's still a lot of colonial influence. I heard a black girl at a public school who suffered racism. She locked herself in a toilet and tried to cut off her skin to make herself white. But when you try to talk about racism, we're told we're neurotic. That's a form of violence. Kids from the *favelas* always attend state schools but they have to work for their families too. Therefore, *favela* kids never have good enough education to get into public universities. They never have a chance. Those places go to middle-class kids from private schools. That's a form of violence too. You know … I'm talking about blacks but the same applies to Indians and whites who have nothing. People say hip hop is all about violence but they don't understand. Rap in this country is very anti-violence and does a lot of good. Of course, it's not the only way to help people, but I know it's helped me. Some people want to change hip hop to 'I love this woman' and all that stuff. But we've heard that so many times in other music and, I ask you, do people really have that much love?[32]

AfroReggae is another example of a hugely popular group that uses music and other performative arts as an entry point into the lives of traumatized youth and children in *favelas*. However, the praxis of AfroReggae suggests that this is not uncomplicated, in that they resort to emulating the disciplinary structures of the drug gangs. Thus, apart from a broader politicized narrative of structural exclusion and marginalization because of official complicity with the profits of the drug trade, especially at the upper circuits of the value chain, the leader of AfroReggae, Junior, knows that he must mirror the discipline and hierarchies of the gang cultures. The point is that he knows that his movement must offer an alternative home and sense of belonging because that is what the gang offers in the first instance, apart from access to financial resources which are not available through participation in the formal labour market. In other words, the solution is not simply a matter of restoring the sense of self, pride and dignity of these young people and then they will somehow, miraculously, manage to stay on the straight and narrow of the alternative lifestyle the movement offers. Again, MV Bill captures this dynamic clearly when he argues:

> They don't have any opportunity of becoming something else; each one is their own judge and can say what is right or wrong but crime nowadays in Brazil has become just another choice; it breaks my heart to say this but crime nowadays has tragically become a great choice for those who are born with no prospects. I am not going to be hypocritical and say the opposite because this is what I've seen, this is the truth and even I have difficulties in saying to someone 'Get out of the drug traffic' because I don't have anything better to offer. And it is not enough to offer charity assistance, kind of small thing, because television shows the good things in life and this is what everybody is after.[33]

In the same breath, MV Bill also talks about his hip-hop organization, CUFA (Central Association of Favelas), which seeks to offer alternatives to young people. What he resigns himself to here is the larger structural factors at work that reproduce criminal economies. He is not so naive to believe that their piecemeal intervention is a solution on its own. Possibly this is why he has recently collaborated with prominent Brazilian anthropologist/criminologist Luis Eduardo Soares to produce a book, *Cabeça de Porco*, and a documentary on urban violence in nine Brazilian cities. The book brings to light the scale and convergence of urban violence in Brazil, and in particular how the perpetrators of the violence in the *favelas* are becoming younger and more extreme. The book is meant as a wake-up call to the Brazilian establishment, and no doubt also a point of mobilization of external resources to back initiatives such as CUFA and AfroReggae. More importantly, this initiative underscores the fact that structural interventions are required to deal with urban violence; interventions that can dovetail with hip-hop-inspired grassroots programmes such as those of MV Bill and educational initiatives in juvenile prisons.[34] Soares is very clear about the kinds of reforms/transformations that are required in response to the question 'Do you think that having access to information, higher education and projects that increase self-esteem could be a way out of violence?'

> Without a doubt. I am convinced of that. In our book we do not forget the importance of economic power, but we stress the importance of inter-subjectivity, symbolism, affection, psychology and culture. Not because that is more important, but because society has not paid them proper attention. We have to offer youth at a minimum what the drug trade offers: material resources, of course, but also recognition, a sense of belonging and of value. In the end, there is a hunger more profound than physical hunger: the hunger for affection and recognition, which raise self-esteem ... I think that repression should be the last resort. Before repression, there is a lot to be done in the way of prevention, such as reinsertion, education, and boosting self-worth. If we want someone to change, we have to provide the foundation. No one changes if he or she thinks that they are worth nothing. Do we want to exterminate poor youth or integrate them? Pardon and give a second chance also means forgiving ourselves and giving ourselves a second chance, as a society. Wouldn't it be great for us to have the chance of escaping from the horrible guilt of having abandoned thousands of children to the fate of picking up a gun?[35]

Soares intimates that there are two issues at stake. One, it is vital not to lose sight of the humanity of poor black youth who grow up amidst terror and, effectively, social abandonment. There is no recuperating this class of (non)citizens for an inclusive urban polity without acknowledging the fundamental need for an affirmation of their personhood. Two, the scale of reform implicates the state. Poor young people will remain confronted with truncated futures as long as the criminal justice institutions of the state are not transformed to embrace a philosophy that treats repression as a last resort. Clearly, hip-hop projects in *favelas* are not in themselves able to address these ambitious tasks. What they do offer is a vital entry point for young people to exercise agency in larger and multilayered political and cultural struggles for both recognition and reform. However, what the voice and artistic practice of AfroReggae, MV Bill, Racionais MCs, among others, suggest is that if poor black youth are to have a meaningful voice it must be on their own terms, and this is precisely what hip-hop registers potentially offer. This means a politics and aesthetics of rage and militant critique of the thinly veiled double standards of mainstream society. In this regard there are many dozens of artists across the South who work in a hip-hop or popular-cultural vein to make sense and get their instigations across, stoking the desires and ambitions of marginalized youth. Furthermore, in the complex aesthetic registers that hip-hop cultures instigate, young people should be encouraged to explore their identities, aspirations and contexts without too much censorship. Creative artistic expression can potentially create a new political language and symbolic register that is meaningful to young people and potentially impenetrable and alienating to elites and middle classes. This is the point. For political engagement to occur the powerful and privileged must be compelled to acknowledge their different cultures and assumptions, which are typically rendered invisible by virtue of being the social norm; only then can they 'make a difference' as part of a larger cosmopolitan politics. Finally, hip-hop registers offer poor young people a platform for establishing various kinds of regional, national and international networks of engagement and mutual support to foster a multi-scalar agenda that brings together multiple local specificities.

Public culture and the word: Sarai and *Chimurenga*

My final example of the power of culturally driven and informed responses to the complexity of urban change comes from India, Delhi in particular. Circa 1998, a small group of activists arrived at a similar sense of unease about the sterility of academic debates amidst a larger mainstream context of urban violence and strife. This situation coincided interestingly with a countercurrent evidenced in 'a quiet rebirth of an independent arts and media scene'. Furthermore, 'new ideas, modes of communication and forms of protest were being tried out and tested in the streets.... The city itself, as a space and as an idea, was becoming a focus for inquiry and reflection, and a provocation for a series of creative experiments.'[36] It was in this dynamic cauldron of change and renewal that the conceptual foundation of a new initiative, called Sarai, took shape. The discursive sign Sarai is drawn from the traditional connotation with places where 'travellers and caravans could find shelter, sustenance and companionship'.[37] Consequently, the contemporary 'Sarai Initiative interprets this sense of the word "sarai" to mean a very public space, where different intellectual, creative and activist energies can intersect in an open and dynamic manner so as to give rise to an imaginative reconstitution of urban public culture, new/old media practice, research and critical cultural intervention.'[38] More formally, Sarai is a physical space and programme of the Centre for the Study of Developing Societies at the University of Delhi. On their website, they define themselves as follows:

> We are a coalition of researchers and practitioners with a commitment towards developing a model of research-practice that is public and creative, in which multiple voices express and render themselves in a variety of forms. Through these practices that range from art practice to publication, academic research to the organization of discursive events, setting up of media labs and creative practices in locality labs in disadvantaged neighbourhoods of the city, reflecting upon the culture of freedom, in speech and in software, we have sought to participate in and cultivate a public domain that seeks to find a new language of engagement with the inequities, as also the possibilities, of the contemporary world. Over the last five years, the Sarai Programme has matured into what could arguably be South Asia's most prominent and productive platform for research and reflection on the transformation of urban space and contemporary realities, especially with regard to the interface between cities, information, society, technology and culture. Sarai has also been a robust platform committed to critical discourse, freedom of expression and the exploration of the relationship between human rights, civil liberties and the efforts to ensure the viability of a democratic ethic with regard to media and information practices.[39]

The Sarai initiative's practice takes the form of rigorous and innovative intellectual work that marks out vital new directions in knowledge production, setting out from the city as it is, with all its contradictions, without reverting to a teleological notion that Delhi is en route from informality to high-end services. Instead, it is clear from a reading of the materials that come from this space that the constitutive density of cultures and complexities cannot be reduced to any coherent narrative, but are rather a series of layers of urban reality that always exceed the medium and languages of representation. Sarai's work makes it clear that the new knowledge economy is as present and influential in the slums of Delhi as it is formative in financial centres such as London or New York. In its various projects and outputs, Sarai represents part of a glimmer of an alternative register and sensibility in thinking about and through the informal, emergent, makeshift and insurgent city that is the true heart of urban life in the global South. It is an indispensable critique and methodology for repositioning thinking and practice about the futures of urban life and citizenship in our globalized era.

A similar, if more modest, cultural ferment has emerged in Africa over the past few years. This is a cultural movement rooted in a radical, underground, counter-mainstream positionality, but focused on the real-life inventiveness of cultural activists across the African continent. Despite its radical positioning, the movement also makes allowances for the vicissitudes of making everyday spaces through deals in a messy world. I am referring to the ground-clearing publication *Chimurenga*, which is put out by an independent outfit called Kalakuta Trust. According to their website,

> *Chimurenga*, a pan African publication of writing, art and politics, has been in print since March 2002. It was founded by Ntone Edjabe. The journal is published on the page three times/year, online monthly and through themed performances called 'Chimurenga Sessions.' The intellectual project has snaked from a Miltonian swamp of murky morality and 'paradigms lost' if not into a Garden of Eden, at least into a more lucid landscape where intellect, integrity and humanity are valid tools for growth. A flowering of organic schools of thought grown in backyard gardens, tilled and fertilized by the fundamentals of humanity preached and sometimes practised.[40]

As a result of this positioning and by dint of sheer determination by the nomadic editor, *Chimurenga* represents one of the most important insurgent perspectives on public culture and critical politics across the diverse spaces of the African continent. The reader can gain the flavour of the energetically crazy and stimulating ambit of the project by considering a few of the themes of past issues of the print magazine: 'Conversations in Luanda and Other Graphic Stories' (an amazing special issue with graphic-novel type short stories from across the South); 'Black Gays & Mugabes' (critique and exposé of homophobia in Africa); 'The Orphans of Fanon'; and, more recently, 'Conversations with Poets Who Refuse to Speak', 'a heady mix of words and images that give voice to silence', according to the editorial blurb.[41] The point about *Chimurenga*, Sarai and Urban Think Tank: Caracas Case is that as we move into the future, the hundreds of millions of youth who will remake the city in their own image will find different and new ways of expressing their unique urban experiences and outlooks; these are the still inaudible voices that urban scholars and practitioners will have to learn to understand if they have any hope of making a difference.

Conclusion

One frustration with a book of this nature is that it is biased towards the formal discourses and representations of urban life that decision-makers and policy activists use to define the nature of problems in order to arrive at decisions about how to address them. In the process the dynamism and rich phenomenology of everyday life – which gives cities their true identity and meaning – is taken out of the equation in order to focus on the materiality of poverty and betterment. However, the paradox is that as long as activists and decision-makers fail to engage with the contradictory and elusive complexity of daily life, especially in unregularized and underserviced areas, they are unlikely to generate appropriate or effective policy responses. On the other hand, constitutive complexity and diversity of particular streets, neighbourhoods, zones, communities and districts in urban areas can be so overwhelming that decision-making is neutralised, because the decision-makers have not yet arrived at a 'complete' understanding of everyday dynamics, or, in democratic terms, because not every interest group has been consulted yet. This is not a paradox that can easily be resolved. However, for me it boils down to a sensitivity to the disjuncture between the assumptions policymakers are forced to make about aggregate conditions and the lived realities they are simplifying; it also boils down to a sensibility of openness to different ways of seeing and responding to problems, because in the teeming diversity of the city there will always be an angle or perspective or experience that one has not considered. This reality should be enough to keep any decision-maker or activist modest about their handle on a given situation or problem.

This chapter has attempted to serve as a necessary diversion to the overall rational policy discussion about the most effective policy imaginaries and interventions available to us to understand and address the challenges of urban development in our unequal global era of interdependence. I now return to a macro-policy alternative to the mainstream approaches to urban development reviewed in earlier chapters, hopefully with an appreciation of the pluralism and open-ended dynamism of cities; of the limitations of overly prescriptive or formulaic policy responses, but at the same time of the necessity of intervention by strong and capable states.

7

Counterpoint:

alternative urban development

In the last two chapters I have explained the dynamic nature of urban political life and the undercurrent of autonomy and sometimes insurgency that animates most cities in the global South. The previous chapter sought to counterbalance the tendency in the literature and policy frameworks on developing-country cities by foregrounding 'hidden' dimensions of everyday survival and engagement to make the city liveable for the majority of people who dwell and move in its spaces. The purpose of this chapter is to return to the more formalistic policy models and frameworks that inform the visions, plans and decisions of urban development, for it is incumbent on progressives to propose alternatives, not simply point endlessly to the brutal workings of neoliberal power.

I come from the school of thought that believes one has to get into the guts of urban institutions and decipher what the political and discursive edge is of those institutions in terms of promoting transformative interventions whilst holding on to the 'constitutive outside' of those very organs of power and discipline. This kind of positioning works on the basis of deep engagement with the dynamic character of governmentality, sensitive to the imperative of institutional expression, and hence the scope for subverting and extending the limits of formal politics. This positioning also accepts that under certain circumstances the forces of conservatism may be so strong that there is little point in working with and through mainstream discourses; instead one should confine one's activism almost exclusively to a politics of opposition, resistance and militant refusal. However, even in those cases, if a politics of opposition eventually succeeds in shifting the terrain of decision-making and power, a moment arrives where certain profound institutional and formalization decisions need to be made about consolidating within the practices of the state particular orientations and practices that will systematically shift the weight of exploitation in the city off the shoulders of the poor and abandoned.

This chapter presents a series of interlocking arguments about how to think and act programmatically to bring more just and inclusive systems into being in the routine functioning of the city. The starting point is a brief ideological mapping of an alternative policy matrix that can serve as a touchstone as activists challenge and incrementally supplant the dominant discourses on urban development critiqued in Chapters 3 and 4. This is followed by a succinct political economy exposition of the underlying drivers of urban inequality, which is meant to moderate overconfident discourses about the prospects and likelihood of full-scale urban transformations. Indeed, the brutal workings of dominant powers in the world remain deeply entrenched and creatively adaptive to foresee a full-scale urban revolution in our generation. However, there are an infinite array of opportunities to refuse, undermine, subvert, frustrate and erode that power, which only begin to matter if one can effectively institutionalize such efforts. Such opportunities will be different and particular in each city and town across the globe, but it is possible to weave together a general tapestry of resistance which can serve as a vivid backdrop to local struggles, always globally and regionally articulated. This chapter presents such a tapestry, with a particular focus on two dominant urban policy discourses, which are ripe for engagement, inversion and redeployment to radical democratic purposes. Throughout, the chapter operates on the basis of my perspective on the relational dynamic of urban politics, expressed in Chapter 5.

Alternative urban development perspective

The holy grail of urban development is the achievement of integrated sustainable human settlements whereby the needs of the present generation are sustainably satisfied without compromising the options and resources of future generations. For example, the Habitat Agenda asserts that the:

> Sustainability of human settlements entails their balanced geographical distribution or other appropriate distribution in keeping with national conditions, promotion of economic and social development, human health and education, and the conservation of biological diversity and the sustainable use of its components, and maintenance of cultural diversity as well as air, water, forest, vegetation and soil qualities at standards sufficient to sustain human life and wellbeing for future generations.[1]

This intergenerational definition premissed on the idea of balancing economic, ecological and social outcomes can be traced back to the Rio Summit and its precursor, the Bruntdland Commission.

An alternative definition of the same issues come from the National Science Foundation Workgroup on Urban Sustainability, who argue for

> a definition of sustainability that focuses on sustainable lives and livelihoods rather than the question of sustaining development. By 'sustainable livelihoods' we refer to processes of social and ecological reproduction situated within diverse spatial contexts. We understand processes of social and ecological reproduction to be non-linear, indeterminate, contextually specific, and attainable through multiple pathways ... Within the terms of this definition, sustainability:
> * Entails necessarily flexible and ongoing processes rather than fixed and certain outcomes;
> * Transcends the conventional dualism of urban versus rural, local versus global, and economy versus environment; and
> * Supports the possibility of diversity, difference, and local contingency rather than the imposition of global homogeneity.
>
> Across the multiplicity of concrete situations, the sustainability of local livelihood practices articulates with global-scale socioeconomic and bio-chemical systems in complex, indeterminate, and poorly understood ways. Recent ecological and social theory proposes that socio-ecological processes comprise non-linear dynamic systems that do not tend to equilibrium.[2]

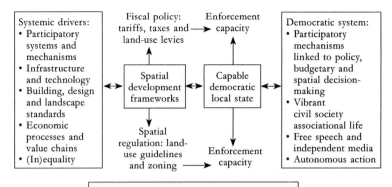

FIGURE 7.I Institutional dimensions
of sustainable urban development

This constructivist approach to sustainable urban development obviously resonates with the theoretical model I explored in Chapter 5. Admittedly, this definition is not the most accessible and easy to understand, but in its focus on process rather than outcome, contingency as opposed to homogeneity, it opens a much more productive line of enquiry about the dynamics and potential of sustainable urban development. Practically, it means that sustainability is consistent with robustness and flexibility in problem-solving within localities, rather than management towards certain, preconceived outcomes. It is often the common drive to predetermined outcomes that hems in democratic contestation because certain urban features become defined as 'world class' and become the de facto focus of local politics, as was demonstrated in Chapter 4. In other words, this definitional approach entails a shift in thinking from achieving set standards and single 'solutions' to empowerment for local problem-solving based on diverse knowledge. Consequently, the role of local knowledge and practice is vital, which suggests that there is much to learn from alternative ways of addressing sustainability in different contexts. But local solutions, conscious of larger power structures and systems of knowledge, need a vibrant political sphere and radical democratic culture to emerge in all their richness. This implies that

'Sustainability is fundamentally a political rather than a technological or design problem, in the sense that the greatest barrier to sustainability lies in the absence of institutional designs for defining and implementing sustainable practices in local contexts.'[3]

The heart of an alternative urban development model is a clearer institutional conceptualization of how to advance more sustainable social and ecological reproduction dynamics within a highly exploitative capitalist economic system that relentlessly produces uneven spatial outcomes that reinforce multiple lines of inequality. This institutional model is best explained with the help of a diagramatic representation (see Figure 7.1).

In this model it is assumed that the preconditions for more sustainable urban lives and livelihoods are: (i) an effective democratic local state committed to a vibrant public sphere; (ii) an effective spatial development framework that can give expression to the developmental objectives of the state and citizens; (iii) a plural, dense and active civil society that engages the state and business sectors around the normative aspirations of the city; and (iv) a (nominal) normative commitment to the right to the city, pluralism, social justice and poverty reduction, which serve as parameters for public discourses about the identity and futures of the city. Of course, where these conditions are underdeveloped or absent, the primary focus of an alternative urban development approach is to bring these conditions to life. In the remainder of this section I will explain the key normative anchors of an alternative urban development model: namely, a rights-based approach and the importance of radical democracy as a preferred model of democratic institutionalization; and what I refer to as systemic drivers of urban sustainability, because these are the practical sites of political struggle that will advance more sustainable lives and livelihoods.

The right to the city

The literature on human rights distinguishes between first-, second- and third-generation rights. First-generation rights typically include civil and political rights; for example, the right to life and political participation. Second-generation rights include economic, social and cultural rights. Third-generation rights are often termed solidarity rights, and include, inter alia, the right to peace or the right to a clean environment.[4] Progressives who adopt a rights-based framework regard these different categories of rights as indivisible and mutually reinforcing.

If one locates the rights-based normative framework in an urban setting, it is clear that various basic services such as water, shelter, waste management and access to energy are found in the realm of the right to life as first-generation rights. This is complemented by political franchise, which in the urban context finds expression in the focus on local democracy and various gradations of participatory governance. These aspects have been the main focus of mainstream urban policy. Clearly the demand for political representation at the local or municipal level and the affirmation of the right to food, water and shelter are crucial for individual and household advancement in the city. But the preoccupation with these basic or first-generation human rights drives international support for transparency in local government elections and for basic infrastructure provision, at the expense of defining a more nuanced and demanding agenda of urban transformation in which more complex rights can be addressed for increasingly large numbers of people who live in the cities of the South.[5] The critical issue is to recognize that a holistic approach that incorporates the full ambit of rights cannot stop with an individual or household focus if translated into a programmatic agenda of the state. In fact, addressing the full spectrum of rights transcends the individualistic dangers of a narrow rights-based discourse and brings to the fore the pivotal role of the state and multi-scalar actions to address the complex interdependencies between different categories of rights.

However, the ongoing focus on electoral and participatory democracy, as well as on protecting other individual rights (freedom from discrimination, freedom of expression, etc.) within mainstream urban development policy approaches, may marginalize new efforts to advance second-generation socio-economic rights. These second-generation rights are achieved through the sustainable ongoing delivery of affordable urban services to households (not individuals) and through viable service administration and finances, not just through infrastructural investment. Hence the emphasis in Figure 7.1 on *capable* democratic local states. How this ongoing service delivery is achieved will vary greatly between urban and rural contexts. What is important to consider, apart from the underemphasis of second-generation socio-economic rights, is a further gap in political commitment and action at the urban scale to provide third-generation rights such as the right to a safe environment, to mobility or to public spaces. These gaps persist despite the fact that many countries have adopted a comprehensive rights approach in their formal constitutions and legal frameworks. For example, the right to freedom of movement, safety, environmental protection and economic opportunity are recognized in both the South African Constitution and the International Declaration on Human Rights. What is significant, though, is that the urban planning and enforcement mechanisms that protect or enable these rights are poorly understood, and hence seldom in place. A vital part of an alternative urban development agenda is to make this lacuna in urban theory and policy visible, and to address it; hence the emphasis in the framework diagram (Figure 7.1) on fiscal and spatial regulatory instruments at the urban scale. In other words, the argument here is that if the full gamut of human rights are to be exercised collectively, and at various geographical scales across the city region (individual, house, property, neighbourhood, municipality and city region), then they must be institutionalized through regulatory systems. Third-generation rights form part of the public good and of what I termed earlier public investment areas (Figure 4.1).

Thus, clearly, implementation of these second- and third-generation rights rests on robust and capable sub-national state structures. Embryonic postcolonial local state structures, unfunded decentralization and privatization all militate against strong urban government in the global South. Consequently, despite obvious wealth being concentrated in large urban areas, the poor are trapped in second-class strata of the city that might one day provide for universal first-generation rights, but will never facilitate full urban citizenship.[6] For me, a rights-based normative anchoring of an alternative urban agenda is helpful because it underscores the centrality of a strong, effective, intentional and democratic local state, contrary to the neoliberal agenda of the past twenty-five years. Furthermore, it brings to the fore in a useful way the importance of articulating, without sublimating, individual and collective imperatives, local and regional scalar dynamics, and cultural, political, economic and spatial imperatives of more just urban development futures. This agenda is usefully and productively summarized under the sign 'the right to the city'. However, a fundamental part of my argument is that the struggles for the right to the city and its incremental realization (and, by extension, institutionalization) is only likely to arise in a context of radical democracy, as explained in Chapter 5.[7]

Systemic drivers of sustainable urban development

The predominant focus on the mainstream urban development approach to slums and strengthening associations of the poor can lead to a lopsided approach that unwittingly (if one is to be generous) creates a context in which the status quo can be reproduced indefinitely whilst the political rhetoric is bloated on feel-good references to sustainability and poverty reduction. Thus, in this section I suggest that the primary focus of an alternative urban development framework must be on the large infrastructure, design and economic systems that account for the routine reproduction of the built environment and the financial and symbolic economies it depends upon.

Participatory systems and mechanisms The now vast literature on participatory democracy makes it clear that in the absence of vibrant, multiple and endowed participatory democratic avenues that can impact on local government decision-making and prioritization, it is unlikely that urban elites will introduce or finance policies that will lead to redistributive or regulatory measures that allow for urban resources to be distributed more equitably. Put differently, in most cities in the global South, extreme levels of inequality and human brutalization through widespread chronic poverty can be tolerated. Unless the urban poor have democratic means by which their interests can be represented and inserted into allocative processes, they will simply be ignored, and urban accumulation policies with only short-term profitability objectives will predominate. Thus, an important and basic conditional urban driver is effective political voice through formal participatory democratic systems. In this regard, the raft of mechanisms and innovations proposed by the Good Governance

Campaign of UN–Habitat is informative even if politically under-qualified, as demonstrated in earlier chapters.

Infrastructure and technology   The contemporary global economic system is clearly anchored in city-regions across the world, with higher levels of aggregation manifested in the traditional triad countries of the North. However, a number of so-called global city-regions in the South are increasingly important nodal points in this multi-scalar space economy – for example, Mexico City, São Paulo, Lagos, Dakar, Johannesburg, Singapore, Shanghai, Mumbai, Bangalore, and so on. It is in these cities, with their very high concentrations of service economic sectors such as finance, insurance, real estate, tourism–leisure, and so on, that the greatest volume of general value-added (GVA) is generated inside national economies; this makes them particularly important and sometimes powerful in national urban systems. The new economic sectors that potentially embody very large volumes of capital rely on a series of particular infrastructures which one can cluster as 'connectivity infrastructures'; these include telecommunications, cheap energy, transportation, and logistical hubs such as ports, freeways and airports. Moreover, the new globalized skilled managerial class that runs these companies that represent the upper end of economic sectors are increasingly seen as demanding leisure and residential infrastructures that can guarantee a hassle-free, insulated, safe, culturally 'rich' (i.e. the highbrow culture of museums, galleries, opera houses, etc.) and insulated existence in cities invariably marked by great social divides. An important evangelist for the lifestyle demands of this small segment of 'world class' cities has been Richard Florida, who promotes the importance of the creative class.[8] The point about all this is that most cities in the global South fall into a trap whereby they come to define their priorities in terms of what they need to do to become 'world class' and competitive, as these sorts of infrastructure investments invariably crowd out public infrastructures that would benefit the majority of urban citizens and affordable basic needs infrastructures for the urban poor. In Chapter 4, I presented a diagrammatic presentation of infrastructure prioritization that tends to respond only, or predominantly, to the needs of the knowledge economy and business interests (see Figure 4.1).

An alternative development approach must be able to put forward a critical argument about urban infrastructure that leads to: (i) a dematerialization of these systems (and the private-sector production processes that feed off them); and (ii) a prioritizing of public-interest and poverty-reducing investment over and above narrow growth-supporting ones. Dematerialization refers to actions taken by industry and the state 'to develop industrial processes that are inherently more benign and [lead to] production and consumption patterns that reduce the flow of matter and energy per unit of economic activity'.[9] Of course, it is not possible to suggest that one can be achieved at the expense of the other, but the alternative perspective is about forcing a debate about the trade-off that has to be made, and to link such a necessarily political engagement back to the normative standards of the city. This debate is becoming increasigly easy to win as private-sector opinion leans increasingly in similar directions.[10] Figure 4.1 depicted the macro balancing-act that urban actors must accomplish as routine decisions are made about what infrastructure will be invested in, maintained and promoted. One can surmise that a progressive coalition of urban actions and networks will address critical economic performance-related infrastructure, but in appropriate balance with adequate levels of investment in public infrastructures and through technological modalities that are increasingly environmentally benign and that improve the labour-market absorptive capacity of the economy. This takes us on to the next two areas of systemic focus.

Building, design and landscape standards   Among the most potent capabilities of the (local) state is its regulatory power with regard to land use, public space regulations, and building standards and norms, which pertain to materials and architectural and heritage-related norms. For example, in the formal economy, building plans typically need to be approved by municipalities, and the criteria for approval can be amended to promote new ways of building and improving the energy and water efficiencies of the built environment. These change drivers also, potentially, lend themselves to multi-class environmental alliances that can build on a sustainable development platform. More importantly, where the local state has a massive public investment drive to provide low-income housing or support for *in situ* upgrading of slums, it can use its own procurement muscle to enforce new standards, which in turn can be used to leverage larger market-wide shifts in consumer and investor preferences. An important example in this regard is, ironically, the neoconservative governor of California State in the USA, whose administration is aggressively promoting solar-based energy solutions for the built environment along with tough emissions-reduction standards for the state and private sector to achieve a 30 per cent decrease in greenhouse gases by 2016.[11] It is fairly obvious that unless the inputs that go into the construction of the built environment are progressively defined in terms of 'dematerialization' criteria it is unlikely that the models of city building will produce the necessary environmental efficiencies to witness a visible reduction in greenhouse gas emissions.

Another closely related progressive imperative that sits at the interface of building regulations, public space guidelines and infra-structural priorities is public transport. Given the insane growth in automobile use in the emerging regions of the global South, especially Asia, it is clear that unless a commitment to safe, widespread and affordable public transport becomes the linchpin in alternative urban development models, it is unlikely that the livelihood prospects of the urban poor will be improved or better environmental outcomes realized. The impressive 'turnaround' in dominant urban design and development cultures of Curitiba and Bogotá remain important reference points for progressives. These cities prove that public transport is a popular, legitimate and achievable platform around which to build broad-based coalitions. Moreover, once the legitimacy of a commitment to public transport is secured politically and reinforced by adequate budgetary allocations, then it becomes much easier to push for more sustainable standards and technologies with regard to energy, solid and liquid waste management and water consumption; all profound systemic drivers of urban exclusion and unsustainable processes.

Economic processes and value chains   Over the decades since the Rio Earth Summit in 1992 there have been profound normative shifts in the domain of private capital. A number of voluntary regulatory frameworks now exist which extend from fair-trade practices to respecting worker rights, and increasingly touch on the imperative of internalizing environmental externalities into the pricing structures of private companies. It seems as if the core argument of environmental economics about the externalization of environmental costs is striking a chord among the 'enlightened' sector of global business leadership as evidenced in the rhetoric spouted at the annual Davos corporate love-fest. It is of course easy to be totally sceptical about the seriousness or depth of these shifts and to write them off as window dressing or a cynical attempt to appeal to shifting consumer sentiments in the North without changing the exploitative logic of capitalist forms of accumulation. I think this is an error. It seems that such an approach fails to appreciate the institutional logic of private firms and how certain shifts in norms and predispositions can instigate profound structural effects that extend beyond the control of any one company.

It is obviously beyond the scope of this book to explore these issues in any depth, except to suggest that there is a lot of scope for principled partnerships and coalitions with enlightened corporate interests that want to position themselves in ethical and environmentally sustainable terms, to the extent that they can improve the working conditions of their employees, with knock-on effects for their suppliers and clients. The point is that once this political agenda begins to internalize environmental costs and influence the entire value chain, the consequences can be far-reaching and potentially systemic. Given the disproportionate power that business needs and interests exercise over urban development priorities in the minds of public-sector leaders and managers, it is vital that activists striving for an alternative urban path exploit the new opportunities for regulation and redistribution that this area allows for.

(In)equality Even though inequality is endemic to capitalist modes of accumulation, it is evident that the level of inequality a particular society is willing to contemplate and tolerate differs greatly, not only between the North and South but also among countries that fall into these two categories. In an urban context, fiscal instruments, redistribution formulas and land-use guidelines can greatly shape the

nature and extent of inequality. One of the most important dimensions of an alternative urban development agenda is to address social and economic inequalities directly by first and foremost adopting progressive taxation systems and then enforcing them with minimal room for corruption. This implies vigilant civil society oversight and mature political leadership.

Fiscal instruments are particularly important in ensuring that urban services are priced on the assumption that the fundamental human rights of all urban citizens make them eligible for free basic services that are essential – drinking water, cleansing, sanitation, shelter from the elements, affordable energy and safety. In contexts with widespread poverty it is imperative that municipal tariff systems are based on a stepped formula whereby the unemployed and poor have free access to a minimum quantum of water and energy, and consumers who can afford to pay for services cross-subsidize the usage of the poor along with the general fiscus. South Africa has made important strides in this regard but has a long way to go to make it adequate for the needs of the poor.[12] The other dimension that perpetuates unequal access to urban resources and opportunities is land markets. It is widely acknowledged that the current form of globally embedded economic development in cities produces greater spatial segregation and social Balkanization. Land-use instruments can go a long way to counteract and ameliorate these effects if local states are politically compelled to arrest and reverse urban segregation and fragmentation. For example, the magisterial review of urban planning instruments by Robert Riddell offers encyclopaedic details on how to achieve more integrated, equitable and sustainable land-use outcomes.[13] So the issue is not an absence of precedent or policy tools but rather an unwillingness on the part of urban governments to deploy these instruments, which in turn can be traced back to insufficient democratic pressure on states to make such recalcitrance very expensive.

The point of this section is to demonstrate that it is possible to think in very practical terms about the primary pressure that can be targeted to shift the underlying drivers of urban systems. However, this approach does presuppose a democratic system of urban governance, opportunities for radical and progressive groups to engage with decision-making and planning processes, and an open public sphere that allows for alternative approaches to be tabled and advanced. It also assumes that guiding instruments in the form of spatial development frameworks inform more precise regulatory tools in the domains of urban financial policy and land-use management. These conditions are clearly not in place in many cities in the global South, which does preclude the possibility of progressives pursuing these lines of radical incrementalism. In those places it makes more sense to opt for advocacy and militant direct action that can lead to the institutionalization of participatory democratic systems. It is becoming very difficult for nation-states with global integration ambitions to eschew formal democracy even if they remain demagogic at heart.

Political economy of urban transformation

At the heart of the crises of urban development described in Chapter 2 is a contemporary dynamic whereby urban spaces are increasingly marked by deeper lines of spatial fragmentation, social and economic segregation, and of course inequality. To capture the systemic nature of these factors, which is left underdiscussed and undertheorized in mainstream policy discourses of the World Bank, Cities Alliances and UN–Habitat, it is important to explore in a slightly theoretical vein how these contemporary features of urban life come to be. This section summarizes understanding in contemporary urban studies of segregation, fragmentation and inequality, and the causes of their (re)production.

In general terms, urban segregation can be seen as an outcome of urban inequality in capitalist cities, which is reinforced by urban management and planning ideas that valorize the ordered fragmentation of urban space. Iris Marion Young provides a useful working definition of segregation and its general causes:

> [S]egregation consists in an enforced separation of groups that confines members of some groups to specific areas, or excludes members of a group from specific spaces, institutions, or activities, or regulates the movements of members of segregated groups ... group based residential segregation is common in modern democracies with self-consciously differentiated groups. Where it exists, it is the product of class and

income differentials combined with a variety of discriminatory actions and policies of individuals, private institutions, and government.[14]

This coincides with the perspective of Savage et al., which regards segregation as the spatial expression of inequality.[15] Inequality can be mapped in terms of differential access to economic resources (wages, land and knowledge) and collective consumption goods and services (i.e. education, health service provision, town planning and transport), social standing (i.e. status) and political power.[16] Capitalism (in all its variants) is fundamentally an economic, social and political system that produces and exploits inequalities in society. In this light, it is clear that inequality is always multidimensional and the various elements tend to operate in a mutually reinforcing manner, linked to (but not fully determined by) the political-economic reproduction of society. It is this character of inequality that makes it a particularly intractable problem. Furthermore, it is impossible to understand the reproduction of inequality outside of an appreciation of how group identities and subjectivities are reproduced in the city, in specific neighbourhoods or enclaves.

Initially, in classical functionalist and structural (Weberian and Marxist) approaches to urban studies, identities were seen in static and deterministic ways. In other words, it was assumed that economic and political forces (e.g. racism) determined the subject position of people – for example, as working class or black working class. These ascriptions of identity, linked to people's relation to the means of production, were seen as adequate to explain subjectivity. Furthermore, '[s]ocial divisions were thus predominantly seen as deriving from economic forces and organized around class.'[17] This approach was uprooted with the introduction of the notion of 'difference' by feminist, psychoanalytical, postcolonial and poststructural theorizations in social theory more generally, and urban studies more specifically, during the 1980s.[18] As a result, there was 'a move away from thinking about identity and subjectivity as static, essential categories, to seeing them as shifting, decentred and multiply located'.[19] In addition to regarding identity as multiple and hyphenated, it is also necessary to recognize that 'identities are also "hybrid", that is, overdetermined, and structured by the unconscious desires in a relation of alterity to the other and the self', as explained in Chapter 5.[20] For this reason, it is impossible to tease out specific dimensions of identity – for example, gender, race or nationality – in pure forms. On the contrary, the various dimensions of hybrid identities are mutually constitutive and shaped by various spatialized experiences – locality (home, street, neighbourhood, city), nation and transnational territories.[21] Lastly, identities are also fluid, always under construction and fundamentally open-ended. The multiple spatialities in the city provide the raw material for the incessant work of making identity in particular places.[22] This theoretical position makes it impossible to read off from a person's residence (e.g. in a ghetto or gated community) or job description (e.g. in a factory, office or as a home-worker) their political and economic interests. Also, it makes it impossible to assume the 'cultural character' of a neighbourhood, based on the class profile of the inhabitants.

Such a nuanced conceptual approach to identity and subjectivity invariably complicates understanding the reproduction of segregation and inequality, because there is always a margin of complicity in the functioning of regimes of difference; for power works through difference to reproduce inequality. With the intensification of awareness of, and attention to, multiplying differences in postmodern societies, urban inequalities – manifested in various forms of segregation – are intensifying.

> Cities, therefore, are becoming places where far from encountering difference, people actively contrive to avoid it. Different social classes, increasingly, are forced to follow different trajectories through space, they inhabit different zones for work and leisure, and rarely, if ever, do they unexpectedly encounter the 'other'. The ideal urban environments are places of control rather than disorder. This city of difference is not a place where diversity is celebrated on the ground. It is a place of watchfulness and suspicion – of enclaves of homogeneity, perhaps even community – a place where mingling with strangers is to be avoided.[23]

Many forces and factors contribute to urban fragmentation and divisions: the operation and functioning of land and housing markets; planning aimed at social control and modernist functionalism; consumer preferences of particularly the middle classes, who seek safety and exclusivity; symbolic and psychic attachments to particular places; the physical form of the city and how it actively prevents certain categories of people (e.g. those with disabilities, or women or children) moving around or accessing services and goods.[24] It is vital to relate these more structural factors to questions of identity and power. 'Different marginalities, such as race, gender, or sexuality, or other forms of exclusion, interrelate to concentrate sites of power disadvantage and are not simply a question of special needs or lifestyle but are embedded in power relations, whether these be symbolic or real.'[25]

In other words, whilst accepting the validity of a difference perspective, which foregrounds the complexity of subjectivity and the relationship between place and identity construction, it is also possible to be clear that unequal power relations operate through spatial differentiation to concentrate a lack of access to bases of power. Where these perspectives often fall short, however, is in relation to the *appropriate* role of public policy in addressing power disadvantage, including that reproduced through the segregation and fragmentation of urban space, leaving deepening inequality in its wake.

Unravelling political opportunity

Driving an urban transformation agenda is much like detective work. Due to the historical depth of urban dynamics, the impact of multiple spatialities that coexist and jostle in the city, and the complex socialities that arise from every shifting term of identity and community, figuring out the most effective routes to a transformative agenda requires painstaking attention to detail with a heightened sense of the political. In Chapter 1 I introduced the idea of the city as a political terrain with various domains of political action. However, to understand the dynamics of each of these domains (and their interfaces), following Patsy Healey, it is useful to pay particular attention to three dimensions of power dynamics.[26]

The first dimension is specific episodes that unfold as a drama that can be read in terms of plot-lines, competing actors and pointed towards particular outcomes with differential consequences for the different actors implicated. In an increasingly globalized world the 'big' episodes that structure attention and a sense of political unfolding – that is, the city's storyline – are typically large-scale investments in freeways, ports, wireless meshes, signature buildings or museums, international sporting events and so forth. These episodes provide a set of clues about where power and influence coagulate in the city – that is, the identity of the actors and the nature of the strategies deployed to secure their interest. At the same time, the episodes that fall outside of public and media attention are equally informative because they point to the moments that pass by unnoticed, and often these decisions are even more revealing about the nature of power relations in the city.

Second, interests in the city are channelled and aggregated through various networks and coalitions that often span the social domains – the state, private sector and civil society – that analysts too easily separate out. The discourses mobilized by these interest-based networks and coalitions provide important clues about how political priorities are framed as a problem statement, which ineluctably leads to particular kinds of solutions. Thus, in many cities today, centrist and right-wing coalitions would present the need to become world class and globally competitive as the primary motivation for everything that gets done in a city. More importantly, these rationalizations would become unquestionable common sense, skewing the bias of democratic and corporatist deliberation forums in the direction of policy recipes that adopt the same assumptions. If progressives are to succeed in advancing the agenda mapped out above, it is vital that they remain vigilant about these tendencies and hold explicit and clear views about how particular policy biases are mobilized and sustained in the city.

Third, Healey reminds us that urban politics are embedded in particular governance cultures where a number of deeply engrained values and informal norms underpin the relationships and behaviour of urban actors. This point is particularly germane if one accepts my argument that urban politics are always deeply relational, shifting/ adaptive and subject to discursively shaped norms in the public sphere regarding what is appropriate at a given moment. It is only with an intimate knowledge of urban political actors, institutions and dominant norms that epistemic communities will be able to successfully advance alternative agendas that reach down to the systemic level of the city. On this note, let me clarify what I mean by epistemic communities, painted here as pivotal change agents in the city yet to come.

Driving urban transformation:
epistemic communities/strategic networks

Given the complexity of building an effective politics that can simultaneously impact on the systemic drivers of the city and deepen democratic institutions, it is appropriate to define my conception of the change drivers that are most likely to inhabit interstitial spaces between the various domains of urban politics.[27]

Ideas matter. Ideas are indispensable for interpreting what is wrong in our cities, how it can be fixed, and what is better than what we are settling for at the moment. Ideas can ignite creative energy, resistance and movements for change. Ideas can also fix the future, creating the conviction that we are trapped by the powers of geography, time and capital flows. Much of the impasse in urban development stems from the incorrect belief that we are circumscribed by very narrow parameters for manoeuvre at this particular juncture in history. This storyline is unconvincing because much can be done to break away from the mainstream tropes of urban development critiqued in earlier chapters. In the earlier parts of this chapter I have not been proposing any particular recipe for urban development (not that recipes don't have their place), but have sought to persuade the reader that *endogenous ideas* can be generated through focused processes of debate and engagement about dealing with the nerve endings of inequality, environmental degradation, and economic and social exclusion. Specifically, my suggestion is that unless more coherent 'epistemic communities' emerge in our cities, we are unlikely to generate the kinds of ideas and creativity that will point the way out of our condition of urban crisis.

The notion of 'epistemic community' is derived from the idea that knowledge-generating collectives can be assembled or networked to enable a vigorous exchange of perspectives within a broader shared commitment to find practicable 'solutions' to intractable social and economic problems. This conception builds, on the one hand, on ideas about the roles of 'organic intellectuals' in society as formulated by Antonio Gramsci, and redeployed by Cornell West, Edward Said and Stuart Hall.[28] On the other hand, it draws on the Aristotelian idea of *phronesis*, as advanced by planning theorists Bent Flyvbjerg, Jean Hillier and Michael Gunder. Phronesis essentially refers to the skill and reason of practical judgement 'in the moment of action'.[29] It is an intellectual virtue that strives to realize good and effective action in complex and unfolding circumstances. In Gunder's approach, it is particularly attuned to unequal power relations and to finding the most pragmatic and strategic path forward to effect urban policy actions that can produce greater equity and social justice.

By making the link between organic intellectuals and the practice of phronesis, one can argue that the purpose of the epistemic community is fundamentally to challenge conventional orthodoxy (the mainstream) about what is possible and not possible in terms of transformative urban development agendas. Expounding on Said's understanding, Ashcroft and Alhuwalia remind us that '[o]rganic intellectuals ... are those who are actively involved in society, striving to change it rather than maintain traditions. Unlike traditional intellectuals who "remain in place", organic intellectuals "are always on the move"',[30] in search of workable alternatives that can become hegemonic. Cornell West develops this idea by casting organic intellectuals as *catalysts* who stay 'attuned to what the mainstream has to offer – its paradigms, viewpoints and methods – yet maintains a grounding in affirming and enabling subcultures of criticism'.[31] This is a vital aspect of an epistemic community's role – understanding the rationalities and governmental technologies of control whilst recognizing its inherent limits and potential for critical subversion to serve more insurgent interests of the excluded and discriminated in the city. One aspect of fulfilling this role is to engage with the totality of urban development policies as encapsulated in municipal development plans or city development strategies and the institutions these planning frameworks are embedded in. Another aspect is to identify the most strategic leverage points to push mainstream development agendas beyond their own limits towards a more redistributive, inclusive and integrated footing, which grafts on to the systemic drivers explored above (Figure 7.1).

There will undoubtedly be the danger that an epistemic community loses its sense of what constitutes creative alternatives that can resonate with present crises, for what is cutting-edge and innovative is profoundly contextual, subjective and generational.[32] It is therefore crucial that an epistemic community remains attuned to its own potential for new orthodoxies and builds into its functioning and identity, the mechanisms for critique, renewal and even termination, if the need arises.[33] An implication of this approach is that such an epistemic community (of organic intellectuals) cannot remain (or even arise?) within the state or in highly institutionalized civil society organizations. It must inhabit a space in the border zones between the state, civil society, the grassroots, academia and the business sector. It must be open to multiple perspectives and practice the art of interpretation and translation in order to bring new meanings and understandings to life. It must keep an ear firmly to the ground in order to know and feel the various pulses of the city and its changing moods.[34]

Fundamentally, an epistemic community is, to my mind, about opening up vital debates and enlarging the public sphere through the projection of iconic ideas, rooted in sound analysis, about viable alternative ways of city building. However, the progressive ideas that emanate from an epistemic community should be embedded in a political framework of strategic action across the various domains of urban politics discussed in Chapter 5. In this way urban development policy counterpoints are placed within a relational chain of actors and agendas that are continuously analysed and calibrated to deal with concrete problems, challenges and hegemonic discourses. In this respect, the biggest challenge is to engage in an informed and intelligent way with economic processes and actors, given the constitutive function of economic well-being in realizing a host of social and environmental objectives. Differently put, along with exploring and foregrounding the cultural complexity of the city there is a need to adopt a political economy lens in identifying strategic actions to address urban inequality and fragmentation. This is easier wished for than achieved, especially during the current moment when neoliberal economic ideas remain hegemonic and entrenched, particularly among government leaders and powerful private-sector interests.[35] However, if progressives and the various epistemic communities in which they embed themselves focus on the institutionalized points of decision-making in urban governance processes, they can achieve progress. In light of this I now turn to the final aspect of institutionalizing an alternative urban development approach in the heart of the city's multiple and overlapping planning systems.

Strategic entry points

In order to justify my focus on urban planning systems as the primary institutional entry point for advancing an alternative urban agenda, I need to make an explicit argument to link my conception of relational radical democratic politics (mapped in Chapter 5) with the drivers of the systemic change perspective, detailed above. This clarification will be followed by a presentation of a typology of overlapping urban planning systems. With regard to the former imperative, the most economical way of drawing the conceptual linkages is to summarize my assumptions as a series of interrelated propositions about the preconditions required for transformative politics to take root in the city.

Connecting the dots

First, effective and adaptive democratic public institutions (local state) must exist. Second, democratic local states will only remain committed or interested in transformative urban policy if there is a growing autonomous civil society sector capable of mobilizing around its (diverse) interests in relation to the state and other power interests in the society. Third, cities require enabling or supportive regulatory environments in order for civil society actors and local state bodies to engage effectively. In the absence of these there can be a fundamental disconnect between the disparate actors, essentially serving the interests of a narrow and probably shrinking elite. Fourth, if an enabling/open environment for local state–civil society exists there is a need for a shared understanding of the issues that are critical for the city's sustainable enhancement or betterment. My proposal is that the systemic drivers discussed earlier serve as fruitful entry points in identifing such critical issues. Fifth, it is vital to structure democratic deliberation on these critical issues of consequence, and embed it in larger symbolic politics that shape the public discourses and the shifting lines of hegemony. Issues of consequence refer, inter alia, to aspects of the underlying drivers of equitable access to urban opportunities, such as suitable and affordable land for the urban poor, quality education, employment and affordable public transport. Sixth, transformative politics require an explicit articulation of local-level struggles around household and neighbourhood reproductive issues and the city-wide issues of consequence that arise from the systemic drivers of urban reproduction. Lastly, planning systems (not exclusively or necessarily) offer a unique opportunity to facilitate local and city-wide articulations because, ideally, planning matrices consider and address long-term structural factors, their spatialities and potential social-cultural embedding in order to achieve traction. Building on these propositions, I will now explore the specific potentialities of planning, having first presented a typology of planning.

A working typology of planning

In the interest of space I use a diagramatic tool to summarize the various types of planning, each with different reaches and impacts on the city (see Figure 7.2). I will now briefly describe each form of urban planning.

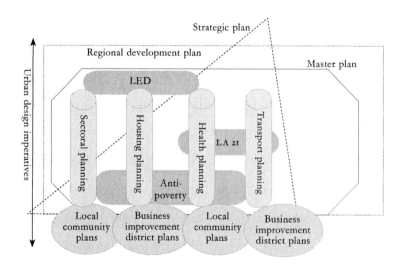

FIGURE 7.2 Overlapping dimensions of urban planning

Master planning   This is the most conventional form of city-wide planning. Typically it is meant to provide a rationale for urban land use and serve as the basis for more detailed zoning systems and codes. The scope and reach of master planning varies from country to country. For example, in Brazil master planning remains a vital instrument to define land use in progressive terms. The Statute of the City, promulgated in 2001, is a potential instrument for redistribution through land-use reforms which define social uses that advantage the poor as more important than economic uses that favour the elite.[36] However, in most countries master planning is largely ignored and only serves to inform land-use provisions at very general levels. Nonetheless, it is important to bear in mind that despite the limited effectiveness of master plans to ensure equitable and sustainable land-use patterns in the city, they remain an important starting point for regulatory systems and land-use provisions that structure urban space.

Sectoral planning   The major functional areas of urban development can be captured here – transport, education, (primary) health, energy provision, water, waste management and sanitation. These services tend to consume the bulk of the day-to-day focus and resources of municipalities. Also, planning in these areas tends to reinforce the departmental silos that continue to characterize most municipal governments. These plans, via departmental champions, also tend to structure the budget of the municipality: each sectoral plan with its respective capital and operating expenditure splits, which makes it difficult to reorient and reposition the underlying drivers of municipal priorities and actions. It is common for sectoral planning to be closely tied to basic-needs-oriented development approaches, policy preferences that tend to be, at best, ameliorative even if important.

Multi-sectoral planning   During the late 1980s and 1990s the importance of more integrated development approaches came to the fore. A forerunner in this regard was the environmental perspective encapsulated for municipalities in Local Agenda 21 strategies, which arose out of the UNCED Summit in Rio de Janeiro in 1992. Since then there has been a proliferation of cross/inter-sectoral policy perspectives that are applicable at city level. For example, local economic development policy frameworks seek to tie together the impact the municipality has on the regional economy it is embedded in as an economic actor in its own right (with a substantial asset base and various forward and backward linkages in the economy) and as a structuring force of various types of markets and their efficiency and equitability. Other multi-sectoral development approaches include: social development, HIV/AIDS prevention and mitigation, poverty reduction frameworks, and, more recently, climate change adaptation and mitigation strategies. These strategic imperatives lead to a different kind of planning that seeks to bring various development imperatives, scales and temporalities together, with a strong emphasis on institutional design implications that either retard or facilitate cross-departmental functioning. It is probably fair to say that multi-sectoral policy frameworks and planning have become commonly accepted, but their actual implementation and embedding in municipal governments remain very limited.

Area-based planning   Another dimension of multi-sectorality has been the rise of area-based approaches to effective poverty reduction or (economic) urban renewal. Much of the urban poverty literature suggests that it is vital for municipalities to recognize the importance of tailoring multidimensional responses to particular local communities/ neighbourhoods, because of the great variety of livelihood strategies that poor communities adopt. This implies an institutional form geared to respond to local specificities in the form of multidisciplinary teams that conduct multidimensional programmes in response to various dimensions of urban poverty, such as health, economic exclusion, access to basic services, transport access, appropriate information about labour market opportunities, and so on. Such area-based interventions usually also require area-based planning and budgeting, which allow for a practical mechanism to pursue multi-sectoral development strategies. The other increasingly common dimension of area-based approaches is the dramatic rise of urban renewal programmes tied to business-improvement districts. In this instance area-based planning allows private-sector interests to pool their resources and achieve higher levels of public services, especially security and cleansing, for the business district within which they operate.[37]

This dimension of planning raises important questions about the potential to connect spatial planning at the neighbourhood scale with larger territorial scales of the city and the broader region it is embedded in. I believe it is the articulation of local, city, and regional scales that can give planning a powerful role in animating a more precise urban and strategic urban politics because it sharpens the questions about the drivers of urban growth, inequality, fragmentation, unsustainability and social divisions. At this point it is appropriate to bring in the role and function of master plans, regional development strategies and strategic planning.

Regional development planning This achieved greater recognition and favour after the worst impact of the Reagan/Thatcher years of anti-planning and the abandonment in particular of comprehensive and master plans. Regional development strategies and plans arose as a response to the infrastructure coordination imperatives that accompanied the spatial effects of increasingly globalized production and value chains, which in turn made network infrastructures and mobility systems crucial to city-based economic competition.[38] Given that the labour-market catchment areas and various economic circuits are stretched across local municipal boundaries, it became increasingly accepted in Europe and the UK that regional planning is an indispensable tool to foster the rationale for inter-agency and intergovernmental coordination, especially after the radical institutional restructuring that accompanied the neoliberal managerialism that reigned supreme in most urban areas across the world during the 1980s and early 1990s.[39]

Strategic planning The other direction that macro-planning took after the height of the neoliberal onslaught against planning was towards a focus on strategic planning. I discussed this at some length in Chapter 4.

Significantly, as one looks across various contexts, it is apparent that all of these diverse forms of planning are couched in participatory discourses that place a lot of emphasis on the processes of conducting and implementing the plans, which in itself represents a range of new frontiers for democratic politics that go significantly further than traditional forms of claim-making to simply register the demands of the urban poor and marginalized. However, if progressive civil society interests merely focus on exploiting the processual potential of the different forms of planning and lose sight of the importance of relating these different parts of the overall urban planning system, then urban politics will remain limited; hence my focus on the role of planning as an *entry* point to move forward a highly strategic politics trained on the drivers of the urban system.

Planning systems as an entry point for transformative urban development politics

Fundamentally, urban politics is about distributive justice. In other words, it is about how public resources are deployed to ensure the effective reproduction of the urban system whilst all citizens are afforded an opportunity to exercise and realize their rights, especially socio-economic rights to housing, health, culture, safety and dignified employment. Commonly urban governance and management systems are not geared to facilitate meaningful agonistic engagements between interest groups and citizens to understand why resource allocation happens in particular ways and why only sectional interests are served by municipal policies and programmes. Instead, one could argue that the uncritical promotion of participatory governance and planning has been so focused on the politics of consensus and its concomitant processes that they have masked the deep-rooted causal drivers of urban inequality and social-ethnic Balkanization.

As I have argued throughout this book, an important precondition for a more radical urban politics is the promotion of dissensus: that is, focused disagreement on how best to allocate public resources across space (different neighbourhoods and quarters of the city) and time (how to stagger and sequence public investment into various categories of infrastructure and services). These fall into the realm of what was earlier referred to as critical issues of consequence. In keeping with radical democratic theory, explored in Chapter 5, the point of dissensus is more to ensure that conflict is not suppressed, but of course at a certain point diverse and divergent actors need also to agree on how to act at a given moment or around particular interventions, even if all differences between them are not resolved.

Keeping this framework in mind, I will now tease out the specific links between planning and democratic decision-making. In the first instance it is clear that planning offers a vital framework and series of moments to explore and define normative horizons to anchor political discourses and debate. Master planning, strategic plans and regional development plans all tend to start with a set of normative principles such as sustainability, integration, social justice, and so forth, in relation to some conception of territoriality. Of course, the devil lies in the detail of interpretation, but it is incontrovertible that such principles do offer important spaces for radical interests to offer their perspectives on how to address the various problems of the city. It therefore becomes vital that social movements and other interest groups of the urban poor link their everyday struggles and demands to these larger normative frameworks and give concrete expression to the deeper systemic changes that will advance their immediate cause. In this way, social movements can build an alternative set of registers and discourses about how normative principles and horizons such as 'integration' or 'sustainability' or 'endogenous development' link to everyday, incremental improvements, expressed in sectoral and community-level plans. In fact, if the formal processes to conduct local-level planning do not exist or are done in a narrow technocratic fashion, grassroots movements can even construct their own, autonomous plans, which become their reference points for engaging in contestation and negotiation about resource allocation decisions.[40]

Following this line of argument, I think it is clear that theorists of urban politics undervalue the potential of community-level spatial planning methodologies to cohere and focus grassroots activism and economies of social care. Given that grassroots politics in poor communities are plagued by inter- and intra-organizational conflicts and schisms which often render local activism ineffective and essentially turned on itself, local patronage-based political practices further exacerbate these tendencies. What community-level spatial planning tools offer is a language and framework for diverse local actors to negotiate, within a spatial register, how their respective agendas and issues relate to one another. Furthermore, it becomes possible also to see what the sequential relationship between various issues may be. For example, the link between campaigns for access to water and campaigns for improved health services in the same community can be framed as one struggle in a situation where home-based care for HIV/AIDS sufferers places pressure on water usage in poor households.

Typically, neighbourhood spatial planning processes attempt to develop a localized vision and argument for what the community needs to find its fullest expression of cultures, resources and (diverse) aspirations. It then proceeds to identify what exists, its quality, efficacy and relevance, and what is absent, for the community to realize its full potential. Local spatial planning processes do work from various assumptions about the basic elements of a viable, vibrant and sustainable community and use such assumptions to structure and direct discussions. For example, there is usually a desire for

> diversity of use – housing, business, shopping, social, cultural and health facilities, offering easy accessibility, opportunity and choice for all; ... a pedestrian-dominated public realm to facilitate a healthy social life and provide an attractive, safe and human-scaled environment; a green-space network that provides accessible open space, with effective water, energy, wildlife and climate management; aesthetic identity that is rooted in the collective identity of the region, reflecting characteristics valued in the community.[41]

Of course, in contexts of abject poverty where slum living and high levels of informality are the norm, it may be too much to expect such expansive development agendas or perspectives to emerge. Nonetheless, even demands for the 'right to housing' and its consequences require one to pay attention to the larger spatial system that expressing the right should be embedded in, which in turn will only expand the remit of political claims and citizenship. Such local city-wide articulations are crucial for a more strategic, ambitious and territorially connected urban politics under the banner of 'the right to the city'. I would therefore suggest that a crucial focus of democratic practice should be spatially framed arguments for what the right to the city means in practice. In this regard it may be an error to dismiss or understate the potential value of various representation tools, such as plans, drawings, illustrations and the like, to capture and express local, co-determined visions. For example, many of the urbanism frameworks I have seen in Brazil that underpin *favela* upgrading programmes in Salvador, Rio de Janeiro and São Paulo embody much of what I have in mind here. My question is, to what extend are social movements using these registers to spatialise their claims and so confront the deeper drivers of urban inequality and social–ethnic Balkanization?

There is, furthermore, a lot of scope to redirect the resources stored in the large sectoral departments of municipalities to the needs and interests of poor neighbourhoods if, through local strategic spatial planning frameworks, community organizations target their lobbying more precisely. Again, with the spread of participatory discourses across the whole gamut of urban development, all sectoral planning models now accept the importance of community engagement and influence over both systems and technologies of delivery and long-term objectives of these services. There is thus a lot of scope to influence the big sector plans – for example, transport, health, education, energy – even if these sector departments are not open to cross-sectoral coordination. What community-level spatial planning brings to the fore is the unavoidability of cross-sectoral coordination because the everyday economic and reproductive functions of neighbourhoods underscore the fundamental interconnection between various inputs such as economic services, health care, public parks, education, transport and so forth. Furthermore, a fundamental shift towards more environmentally sustainable urban infrastructures starts with community-level experiments which establish technological viability and provide the reference points for larger processes of behavioural change.

Planning reform can come from either the top or the bottom but is most likely to involve both dimensions. What is obvious is that the tools and registers of various types of planning are thick with potential to be mobilized for democratic engagement on questions of urban transformation. Planning potentially renders the underlying drivers of urban life more visible, and therefore subject to discourses of change to achieve more fundamental reform of our cities. However, as the disappointing history of urban planning reminds us, there is nothing intrinsic to planning that produces better urban outcomes. Such outcomes have to emerge out of skilful articulation of urban struggles that draws on planning for its potential uses, as intimated earlier, but always located within a much broader repertoire of strategy and tactics.

Conclusion

Radical urbanists find themselves in a paradoxical moment. On the one hand, almost all of the central normative positions about social justice, sustainability, democratic participation, and so forth, have been accepted by the mainstream. On the other hand, whilst this door is open, the imperatives of hard-nosed (neoliberal) models of urban management and citizenship in a cut-throat globalized economy mean that urban conditions, particularly economic and social inequalities, are getting worse. My argument in this chapter has tried to transcend this paradox. I defined the normative framework, anchored in the symbolically rich discourse of the right to the city, and linked that to concrete pressure points that can alter at a systemic level the logic of urban processes. In this, the suggestion was that progressives need to go much further with alternative policy proposals about how specifically – that is, in technological, fiscal, spatial and institutional terms – these systemic drivers can be redefined in order to make alternative urban futures material realities. However, they are unlikely to succeed with this task if they fail to appreciate the constitutive nature of political power and interests in the city; an insight that forces the calibration of alternative policy agendas with street-smart political strategies. In the next chapter I concretize this argument even further by homing in on urban poverty.

8

Making a start towards
alternative city futures

You must understand that this is a place of high intention. This is a
city where they mend torn sails, or souls; hammer hearts back into
place; make fine adjustments in the eye; replace the mind's printed
circuits. Where they roll the projector lens slowly till all the blurred,
shapeless forms snap into focus. But it is also an insupportable
mean, petty place, just as the upswept dark corners of our hearts
are mean and petty, with hard grey floors, bare walls, windows that
will not open ... Some light must always shine behind our lives; but
here it is very difficult for that light to get through.[1]

Irrespective of how difficult and brutal contemporary cities may
seem, there remains a great deal that we can imagine and do to alter
dramatically their future prospects. Progressives have access to a vast
reservoir of ideas, policies, strategies, sensibilities and experiences to
apply to the important challenge of letting the light pierce through
the darkness of dominant trends with regard to urban development
across the global South. In this final chapter I will pull together the
overall argument of the book and home in on what progressives
can do to tackle urban poverty, in particular, and, more generally,
to bring lasting transformative change into the dominant reproduction of cities. Hopefully, by the end, it will be clear that we cannot
escape the rebus character of the contemporary city. Nevertheless we
can certainly make enough momentary sense of it to find the more

opportune pressure points across our city systems to advance more sustainable livelihoods and lives. This is an intellectual and political imperative that haunts us, for we are all, in millions of tiny ways, the cities we desire or dread.

Redux: the core argument

The last three chapters have made it abundantly clear that it is a formidable challenge to combine the sensibilities of radical incrementalism and recursive empowerment. It became clear that one requires a fine-grained institutional and political analysis of the local state (within its intergovernmental context), civil society formations and diverse business sectors. Unravelling the tendencies and practices of actors within these broad categories ineluctably leads to a complicated picture which is rendered decidedly complex once practices are defined in relation to larger political-economic, environmental and cultural systems; all of which display more intense rates of change and reconfiguration as globalizing dynamics become increasingly a driver of urban interactions and decisions. Nonetheless, amidst this complexity and ever-changing scenario, I suggested that progressives who want to bring more just and inclusive cities into the world need to focus their attention on the systemic drivers of urban development: the political system of decision-making and resource allocation; infrastructure; technological standards and systems; building, design and landscape architectural standards that frame the form of urban development; the production systems and infrastructural implications of economic activity in the city-region; and fiscal, service and income-based measures to tackle urban inequality as enshrined in law, policy and regulations of public agencies.

The drivers can be redefined and respecified towards more just purposes if democratic institutions work, especially if there is a capable state and an explicit rights-based policy mandate. However, contrary to the good urban governance policy model of UN–Habitat, I argued that it is not enough to have democratic systems and a formal commitment to human rights. What is required is vigorous democratic contestation, which may involve momentary consensus on policy priorities, but may not, especially if policy forums of deliberation constrict participation and simply reinforce elite perspectives on urban development. Consequently, throughout, there has been a careful argument for vibrant politics that understand different domains of political practice that can be mobilized and articulated in various ways depending on the political opportunity structure of the city, which in turn flows from the dominant discursive formations that frame what is subject to democratic scrutiny and what is not. If that space is very narrow and technocratic, it is then incumbent upon progressives to opt for a militant politics of refusal and symbolic contestation to bring the city to the brink of crisis or political deadlock as a lever to shift the terms and focus of political discourse. Where there is sufficient democratic space, it is incumbent upon progressives to offer alternative proposals on how the drivers of urban change can be thought of and constructed in order to have more just and inclusive outcomes. Furthermore, if such a political space exists, progressives need to target the various domains of the planning system where primary allocative decisions are taken, which are later on codified in budgets and infrastructure investment decisions. This approach rests on a deep appreciation of the political and of the inevitability of institutionalization when it comes to the governance and transformation of cities, especially where there are large swells of poverty and exclusion of various kinds.

Considering the general situation of rising poverty and inequality in most cities in the global South, despite a concomitant rise in formal rhetoric about economic inclusion and greater democratization, it is appropriate to use this last chapter to focus more concretely on the question of urban poverty. Thereafter I conclude the chapter and book with a stylized model of how progressive epistemic communities and the movements they are embedded in can systematically bring transformative change to life amidst the perplexing brutality, violence, inventiveness, pleasure and productivity of everyday life in contemporary cities.

Multidimensional urban poverty reduction agenda

In light of the humanitarian crises that characterize the growth of contemporary cities, as evidenced in the incomprehensible scale of one billion people being forced to eke out an existence in slum conditions, it is obvious that urban poverty must be the primary frontier in the struggle for more just city futures. Debates in academic and policy communities over the past two decades have converged on the idea that poverty is much more than merely insufficient income and goes to the heart of what full citizenship may mean in a globalizing world. Thus, in broad brush strokes, urban poverty can be defined in the following terms.

> Poverty exists when an individual's or a household's access to income, jobs and/or infrastructure is inadequate or sufficiently unequal to prohibit full access to opportunities in society. The condition of poverty is caused by a combination of social, economic, spatial, environmental and political factors. Due to the multiplicity of causal factors and their spatial dynamics, individuals and households may move in and out of poverty depending on stages in life-cycle and shifting political economy patterns. Poverty is therefore much more than a lack of adequate income.[2]

Building on this definitional framing, there is broad agreement that urban poverty can only be reduced and potentially eradicated if a variety of interventions are pursued in tandem, which include, in particular, the coalescing of political power advocating for the interests of the poor. At the risk of oversimplifying a vast and continuing debate, I want to propose a typology of poverty reduction actions (Box 8.1):

1. Facilitating access to good-quality employment and economic opportunities.
2. Increasing the physical asset base of the poor – land, housing, equipment for economic enterprise.
3. Facilitating access to basic services for the poor, including water and sanitation, solid waste management, affordable and safe energy, transport, education, health and shelter.
4. Strengthening the community's management of its own initiatives and external programmes and ability to self-organize. (The most important plank of anti-poverty interventions for CSOs is to facilitate the autonomy and empowerment of poor households and organizations of the poor – community management.)
5. Enhancing democratic participation by the poor in public decision-making to ensure effective monitoring and influence over public resource allocations and service delivery.

6. Ensuring the poor's access to legal entitlements and security.
7. Ensuring access to safety nets to strengthen ability to manage shocks and stresses.

There is a coherence between these seven platforms: activities in 1 and 2 relate to economic dimensions of poverty, whereas activities in 3 and 4 relate to material dimensions and 4–7 relate to political–social dimensions of poverty. Box 8.1 spells out a typology in terms of each of the seven platforms of action.

It is important to recognize that these interventions must be located within a larger model of change that draws explicit links between the micro- and macro-drivers of economic, political and social life. In other words, it is not adequate to focus simply on local or urban policies that address each of the seven areas of poverty reduction work without addressing the articulation between local forces and global dynamics.[3] Thus, local interventions must explicitly contribute to national, regional and global transformation agendas that seek to redistribute decision-making power over questions such as trade rules, environmental standards, labour standards, and so forth. Put differently, urban policy is always, also, national and global policy. However, for now I want to focus on the micro-aspects of poverty reduction in order to paint a more dynamic picture of what is required within poor communities and their cities to advance a poverty reduction agenda. This is influenced by the fact that I have also devoted the earlier chapters to the dynamics and function of macro urban institutions, particularly the local state as it functions at the scale of the city and its adjoining regions.

BOX 8.1 Typology of poverty reduction domains[4]

1. Facilitating access to good-quality employment and economic opportunities (income poverty).

   • Ensuring macroeconomic policies – monetary, fiscal and exchange-rate policies – prioritize the needs of the poor.
   • Ensuring these economic policies prioritize and promote the interests of the poor and informal sector: private investment policies; micro-finance policies; competition policies; labour

market policies; trade policy, especially in the pro-poor sector; financial-sector development programmes; pricing policies.

- Expansion of quality education, especially skills development initiatives.
- Labour-based approaches to public works and/or community contracting for infrastructure and service provision and management (e.g. municipal–community partnerships).
- Enabling policy framework to support and promote the informal sector (e.g. appropriate regulatory framework, land, infrastructure, access to finance and markets).

2. Increasing the physical asset base of the poor: land, housing, equipment for economic enterprise (asset poverty).

- Ensuring that sectoral and cross-sectoral/integrated development frameworks and plans facilitate an increase in the asset base of the poor. Sectoral policies would include those pertaining to land, housing and enterprise development.
- Investment in public spaces of collective consumption to ensure the presence of beauty and greenery in poor communities, which can encourage new forms of sociality and trade and induce collective pride.

3. Facilitating access to basic services for the poor: water and sanitation, solid waste management, affordable and safe energy, transport, education, health and shelter (capability poverty).

Education
- Eradicating illiteracy through outreach activities and national campaigns.
- Ensuring full access to pre-primary and primary schooling through adequate budgetary allocations, quality monitoring of schools, targeted subsidies to ensure full enrolment, devising practical initiatives to reduce gender discrimination.
- Enhancing parental involvement and management of schools and sufficient accountability.

Health
- Full access to primary health-care facilities for the poor.
- Ensuring parental education and enrolment.
- Providing access to safe water and sanitation.
- Promoting breastfeeding and access to health services, including immunization.

- HIV/AIDS programmes.
- Communication strategies to ensure awareness among the poor about health and safety rights and facilities.
- Nutrition programmes (feeding and parental education).

Water and sanitation

- National policy to ensure the poor have access to a minimum lifeline service to guarantee basic daily domestic levels.
- Community-based infrastructure and maintenance initiatives to keep costs minimal for the poor but ensure full access.
- Basic lifeline for survivalist economic initiatives of home-based enterprises.

4. Strengthening 'community management' or organization of own initiatives and external programmes and ability to self-organize. Vibrant community organizations provide an indispensable platform for collective actions to exercise rights, manage conflict in democratic ways and provide a learning laboratory on democratic citizenship – all of which can increase stocks of social capital. Community management is facilitated through initiatives that:

- Strengthen community management capability.
- Support democratic processes internally and externally.
- Focus on organizational development, training and capacity-building.
- Focus on leadership development, especially among women and youth.
- Provide access to useful information in appropriate formats.
- Support collective action aimed at increasing access to opportunities and entitlements; and transforming the policy framework that shapes the opportunity structures of the poor.

5. Enhancing democratic participation by the poor in public decision-making to ensure effective monitoring and influence over public resource allocations and service delivery.

- Proactive support measures to enable poor households and representative organizations to participate in formal participatory mechanisms, especially at local government level.
- Ensuring good governance practices – transparency and accountability – meet the needs of the poor.
- A strong and effective local government system that can ensure the provision of an integrated package of basic services to the poor, tailored to neighbourhood dynamics.

- Improved budget management and transparency, with disaggregated information about expenditure targeting the poor.
- Information and public dialogue tailored to needs of the poor.
- Targeted anti-corruption and anti-abuse efforts in the public service that interface with the poor.
- Actions to expose and address gender discrimination.

6. Ensuring the poor's access to legal entitlements and security.

- Fair judicial system that meets the needs of the poor.
- Providing squatters and landless communities with tenure to reduce the risk of eviction and increase the value of assets, and so raise the prospect of accessing credit.
- Ensuring access to relevant information about human rights, socio-economic rights and the right to information and quality service from public-sector officials.
- Access to information about legal instruments to ensure employment protection and workplace safety and security, especially for domestic workers and other vulnerable categories.
- Protection against violence and insecurity at household and community levels.
- Opportunity and facilities to exercise political democratic rights and responsibilities via adequate arrangements for elections, political representation and accountability.

7. Ensuring access to safety nets to strengthen ability to manage shocks and stresses.

- Access to risk-management mechanisms, e.g. micro-credit and safety-net programmes (e.g. public works).
- Access to emergency curative care.
- Actions to reduce domestic, gender and community violence (e.g. community policing).
- Measures to mitigate environment disaster risks (e.g. better designed infrastructure).
- Spending on and targeting of safety-net programmes, including nutrition, disability, old-age pensions and child support grants and ensuring access to private maintenance grants.
- Emergency credit facilities for the poor in times of disaster or rapid economic decline.

Micro anti-poverty actions

Anti-poverty action at a micro scale involves a wide spectrum of development work, as Box 8.1 intimates. Alan Fowler[5] has usefully summarized both micro- and macro-interventions that are essential to shift the development landscape to a degree that poverty will be eradicated; an end-state he typifies as 'socially just and sustainable economies with accountable, inclusive systems of government'. The micro-tasks involve a range of interventions and services to achieve three broad outcomes:

- empowerment of poor communities and individuals;
- strengthening of local institutions;
- sustained improvements in the physical well-being of poor and abandoned citizens.

This list clearly coincides with the seven anti-poverty planks of action summarized in Box 8.1. The important dynamic to understand is that the first and last outcomes depend on the second – the strengthening of local institutions. This goes back to what we know from the participatory development literature: unless development processes are owned and driven by the so-called beneficiaries, they are unlikely to succeed over the long term. In different terms, the primary task of local development work is to foster strong, democratic, transparent and responsive organizations that enable poor citizens to pool their energies and mobilize for better access to development opportunities and greater influence in the larger public sphere of the city.

However, decades of experience and learning across the South have taught us that people do not participate in collective organizations unless they speak to immediate needs, fulfil identity-based aspirations and serve a political function. Choices to participate or not are heavily influenced by perceptions about the nature of 'political space' to organize and act autonomously from the state and political movements linked to the state. Furthermore, democratic organizations of the poor are very hard to build and sustain, because they are often hijacked by 'local elites', who act as gatekeepers and spokespersons for the local community. For these and many other reasons (that extend beyond the scope of this chapter and book), intermediary service organizations (NGOs) play an important role in encouraging and supporting the formation of democratic movements and mutual-help organizations in poor communities. However, the entry point to foster collective action and solidarity tends to be a specific problem/issue, typically rooted in a sectoral development focus – for example, health, access to credit, access to land, and so on. Numerous sectorally defined examples are listed in Box 8.1, which should help to visualize this point.

The recent debate on sectoral, or fragmented, versus integrated development has highlighted the problems of sectoral-based approaches to development and poverty reduction.[6] The singular lesson that emerges from these debates is that local-level interventions need to address concrete needs or wants, but the processes of addressing needs must also unlock a wider set of developmental dynamics that can visibly contribute to the strengthening of local institutions and empowerment of communities and individuals. Furthermore, in urban contexts dominated by the lack of work or access to productive opportunities, this is often the primary trigger to unlock developmental processes in poor communities. Experience and research, furthermore, suggest that fostering *savings* that are collectively held is often the most effective way of stimulating access to productive assets and employment opportunities. There is a more expanded argument behind this assertion that I can only touch on superficially here. For now, the diagrammatic summary in Figure 8.1 will have to suffice to illustrate the key points. (I link these community-level imperatives to the typology presented above.)

Figure 8.1 makes it clear that the biggest asset a poor community has is its stock of social capital that allows it to carry out collective actions on the basis of solidarity. Social capital is best enhanced through collective actions that address the physical well-being of the participating people (and households) in one form or another. The experience of achievement that comes from positive collective action provides a useful foundation to promote political agency aimed at powerful local actors and the government, depending on the issues at hand. The example of Shack/Slum Dwellers International, discussed in Chapter 6, captures this dynamic forcefully. The central point to take away from this discussion is that effective anti-poverty action

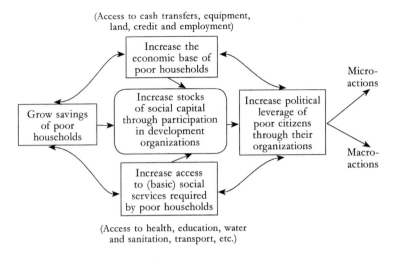

(Access to cash transfers, equipment, land, credit and employment)

Increase the economic base of poor households

Grow savings of poor households

Increase stocks of social capital through participation in development organizations

Increase political leverage of poor citizens through their organizations

Increase access to (basic) social services required by poor households

Micro-actions

Macro-actions

(Access to health, education, water and sanitation, transport, etc.)

FIGURE 8.I   Developmental linkages at the micro scale[7]

at a local neighbourhood scale must combine a degree of sectoral specialization with an awareness of fostering integrated development. Institutionally, this implies that service providers (NGOs), agencies of the state and local associations need to work in a more coordinated manner. Local interventions also require a sharp understanding of how the specific action will link up with contiguous processes at the meso and macro scales. In other words, how do the experiences of local development processes with all their frustrations and achievements directly inform advocacy and lobbying processes at national and international scales? This is the intersection point where the micro *informs* the macro, and where the macro can, potentially, *enable* local action to empower poor households, citizens and their organizational formations.

Tipping points of urban transformation

Just and sustainable city futures need not simply be a utopian aspiration. Champions of the unequivocal 'right to the city' for all have a large and rich canvas with which to work, as I have been at pains to illustrate throughout this book. In fact, we have never before been in a position where the nominal discourses of mainstream institutions are so close to our agenda for justice, equality, inclusivity, sustainability and cultural fulfilment. The problem is that progressives tend to fall into one of two kinds of trap: either they assign everything to the realm of dominating power, manifested in tendencies by governments and development agencies to use progressive-sounding discourses to simply camouflage new forms of rule and oppression; or they uncritically buy into the familiarity of left-sounding discourses and assume that a neat consensus-driven politics will bring redistributive politics and outcomes into the world. What I have been proposing throughout is that the history and spatiality of cities throughout the global South are too dense, specific and redolent with contradictions to lend themselves to such easy readings, no matter how compellingly one marshals the evidence. It is therefore imperative to take the uniqueness and ordinariness of all cities very seriously and think through a prism of radical democracy to identify the unique interventions required to advance radical incrementalism and recursive empowerment, both of which have a deep institutionalism to them.[8] In this concluding section I want to think through the procedural aspects of this agenda.

My starting point is a commitment to radical democracy that finds expression in vibrant political contestation across the five domains of urban politics: formal representative systems; corporatist deliberation forums; sites of direct action by autonomous civil society actors; practice-oriented interventions aimed at enhancing and expanding the livelihoods of the poor and marginalized; and, very importantly, the symbolic domain where competing discourses clash and morph into new imaginaries about the city. The articulation of these domains tells us something about the quality of urban democracy and the room for manoeuvre for progressive agendas. I have proposed further that the city is an ideal breeding ground for various epistemic communities that seek to work at the untidy seams of mainstream urban politics in order to identify vulnerable points, so as always to push boundaries and institutionalize ever more just and inclusive policies that find expression in the regulatory systems of urban governments, especially their budgets and land-use provisions. This is the arena of radical incrementalism signalled in the opening chapter and expounded in the previous chapter.

However, radical incrementalism has little prospect if civil society organizations that represent and champion the diverse interests of the poor are weak, unorganized and ineffectual with regard to formal centres of political and economic power. It is therefore important to stress that my understanding of a dynamic urban democracy rests on the idea that civil society organizations among the poor exist and are autonomous from the overbearing influence of dominant political parties and vested economic interests.[9] Furthermore, it is important that such civil society organizations consciously deepen their own reflexivity and critical practice, because their ideological and political integrity is directly linked to their internal democratic practices and cultures.[10] Patriarchal and authoritarian organizations of the poor will remain limited in how far they can advance transformative agendas for the city as a whole, and will often remain vulnerable to co-option by elites. Typically, these organizations also need to be reasonably adept at generating resources to fund their activities, which again signals something about their capacity to embed themselves in local needs and be seen as relevant by ordinary citizens. Lastly, if these organizations are to be effective they obviously need to be visible in the public sphere. Often organizations representing the interests of the poor render themselves invisible and insignificant because they restrict the ambit of their work to the immediate issues in a particular locality without drawing practical links to the larger city-wide dynamics that cause or reinforce local problems, or they do not invest in symbolic expressions of their work.

So, let us assume a context where there are numerous progressive networks and epistemic communities focused on driving and deepening systemic urban change across a plurality of fronts within a democratic framework which holds the potential to be pushed in a radical democratic direction. In this setting, I would argue that the first task of progressive coalitions is to identify the top four to six 'tough issues' that many actors in the city agree represent the most formidable obstacles to resilient and sustainable urban futures. This could be the prevalence of HIV/AIDS, which is rendered insurmountable because of the pervasiveness of poverty, poor education infrastructure, food insecurity, limited social capital and a persistent resistance among the urban elite to allocate sufficient resources for greater income equality, higher levels of access to basic services and increased expenditure on primary health-care infrastructures and personnel. Or it could be the pervasive presence of extremely violent, patriarchal and, paradoxically, welfare-oriented drug-based gangs that constitute the dominant form of governmentality over territories in the city where, predominantly, the poor live. Whatever the tough or stubborn problems may be, addressing them will require considerable resources, a multidimensional response, an intergenerational agenda and large-scale mobilization of the affected communities themselves.

Once these issues are strategically identified as the most pressing and intractable, they can then be used as a focus to shift the ways in which these problems are conventionally defined and dealt with. This implies a capacity to isolate and expose the primary tenets of mainstream discourses (of the state, business sector and particular civil society organizations) and their effects in terms of resource allocation, likely impact on the problems, and legitimacy in the public domain. Once discourses are deconstructed and revealed for what they actually mean and produce as a societal response, it becomes possible to provide alternative perspectives on the underlying reasons for the disjuncture between the ostensible objectives of the set of policies promoted by such discourses and the probable outcomes. The critical literature on the future prospects of curbing and reversing slum formation is a sobering reminder of just how wide the gap is between dominant discourses and the material impacts of associated policies.

This kind of critical deconstructive work is only the beginning, though, and must lead to serious and rigorous exploration of viable alternatives that may not be able to remedy the chronic weaknesses of mainstream policy solutions but can at least offer some stepping stones to more effective alternative interventions. However, this does imply that progressive coalitions and networks must be sufficiently schooled in the technical and institutional dimensions of mainstream policy approaches so as to identify fairly precise interventions to reposition the energies and resources of the state. Too often, radical scholars and activists are brilliant at critiquing why mainstream approaches fail despite having formally good intentions, but can seldom suggest alternative approaches rooted in the messy and intractable sticky ground that arises from highly asymmetrical capitalist production and social reproduction systems. It is against this imperative that I offered in Chapter 7 the coordinates of a an alternative urban development schematic, because it is around the systemic drivers of the urban system that progressives need to do more spadework to demonstrate how, in particular contexts, the urban can be remodelled, resourced and reorganized along more inclusive, as opposed to exclusionary, lines. Both literature and practice are clearly on the rise across the global South, but more theorization and experimental application are required in order to point the way to large-scale systemic change.

Once alternatives are more precisely delineated to the extent that they can become the raw material for progressive coalition politics, it will be important to take stock of the organizational and institutional capabilities within the (local) state and civil society organizations linked to the urban poor. This task is twofold. First, care must be taken not to overload or overburden the local state with too many imperatives and policies so that it ends up terminally incapacitated because the urban transformation agenda is simply too large and complex to implement in practice. In other words, it is vital that there is a fit between the transformation agenda and the institutional capacity of the state to execute (new) dominant policies and programmes. For example, many scholars of local governance and urban development in South Africa have come to the conclusion that the urban transformation agenda has suffered under the weight of an overgrown and overambitious reform agenda which has produced perverse outcomes, such as the exacerbation of urban sprawl, racial segregation and inequality.[11] Similar suggestions are beginning to surface in the Brazilian urban literature as well.[12]

Second, the task is about understanding whether there is a sufficient critical mass of leaders and activists across the institutional entities to carry forward a complex, critical politics; one that must eschew the temptation of narrow like-minded coalitions, as envisaged in the CDS approach of the Cities Alliance, in favour of a more dynamic matrix of conflicting tensions that produce a higher quality of argument, engagement and practical experiment with more ambitious interventions that act on the nerve endings of urban inequality. The point is that once the appropriate interventions are clarified, it is important to define and strengthen the institutional vehicles and mechanisms to ensure consistent implementation. Urban transformation will not become a material reality without the mundane, almost boring, routine actions of stable institutions that deliver appropriate and quality services at the right scale and in an appropriate sequence to a highly stratified and adaptive citizenry. Getting this aspect of alternative urban development right is as important as figuring out more just and sustainable urban infrastructure solutions or new economic sectors that can generate meaningful employment.

Finally, discovering the unique alchemy of a radical, alternative urban political agenda is about holding on to a strong cultural sensitivity for the numerous and ever-changing rhythms of the city, which never cease to bring fresh and surprising novelty into its very heart. Moreover, a cultural acuity is vital to figuring out what constitutes the most strategic or finely balanced tipping points in the city likely to take it on to a qualitatively different plain in terms of the possibility of transformative change. In my mind, these tipping points come into focus when progressives triangulate: (i) understandings of the main 'tough issues' in the city; (ii) where in space these issues intersect most acutely or visibly to become a focal point for intervention; (iii) where institutional desire and capability reside in the state and civil society; and (iv) imaginative (symbolic) responses arise directly from uniquely local idioms, practices and traditions, which can be remoulded to construct a locally recognizable campaign for transformation. I have expanded in much greater depth elsewhere on how this can work in cities marked by high levels of inequality and diversity, which I shall not repeat here.[13]

Echoing the sensibility of James Sallis at the opening of this chapter, it seems to me that the scope for grounded, radical but necessarily incremental urban transformation is vast; but our ability to exploit that scope depends on our willingness to step beyond a narrow, reactive, interminably critical posture, to one where we take responsibility for letting the light shine through the darkness that engulfs our cities.

Notes

Chapter 1

1. Calvino 1997: 44.
2. The term 'global South' refers to countries that do not have fully indus-trialized economies, largely non-OECD countries with the exception potentially of Mexico, Korea and Turkey. In postcolonial theoretical terms it denotes countries that have experienced some form of colonial domination (directly or indirectly) in their modern history, which have left indelible scars on their economic, cultural and political landscapes.
3. Davis 2005: 202.
4. A quintessential expression of this mode of policy confidence can be found in Jack 2006.
5. Cornwall and Brock 2005.
6. See: Bayat 1997, 2000; Benjamin 2004; de Boeck and Plissart 2004; Roy 2005; Roy and Alsayyed 2004; Simone 2004; Watson 2007.
7. Simone 2004: 11.
8. An important body of work that picks up on a research approach fitting for such readings can be found in Flyvbjerg 2001, 2004.
9. Roe 1993: 93. Technically, Roe distinguishes between the following dimen-sions of complexity: 'the number of components in a system, the degree of differentiation in components, and the degree of interdependence between components ... The most important characteristic of complexity in Demchack's words, is "that complexity produces surprise"' (93–4).
10. Byrne 2001: 11.
11. Here I have in mind the approach taken in Sharp et al. 2000, and the erudite intervention by Amin and Thrift (2005). An interesting attempt

to question the totalizing tendencies of some Foucauldian interpretations of power can be explored in Barnett 2005.

12. See Moore 1994: 123.

13. For a useful account of what the 'good city' may mean in the contemporary era, see Amin 2006.

14. Hall 1996: 244.

15. These ideas are persuasively developed in the various writings of Arjun Appadurai (2002, 2004) whose work seeks to capture the indeterminate dynamics of processes of identity formation and agency in some of the harshest urban contexts in the world.

16. David Harvey (2006) convincingly maps out the reasons for the virtual impossibility of economic alternatives emerging. Adrian Atkinson (2004, 2005) develops this proposition more extensively in recent essays.

17. Lingis (1994, 2004).

18. I have explored these themes in greater detail in Pieterse 2004.

19. I will return to this framework in Chapter 5, but see also Pieterse 2005.

20. There is obviously a lot more to be said about the richness of this framework and the wealth of issues that it will generate if applied systematically to a particular development issue or if one wants to track the governance culture of a municipality over a period of time. We leave it to the interested reader to read the original texts and explore the analytical possibilities (see Healey 2004, 2007).

Chapter 2

1. Satterthwaite 2007.

2. Graham and Marvin 2001.

3. UNFPA 2007.

4. UNFPA 2007: 7–8. It is important to heed David Satterthwaite's (2007) caution that urban projections that go too far into the future, e.g. 2030, must be treated with great circumspection because the underlying data sets for many developing countries remain extremely problematic. Throughout this book I will assume that this warning is understood and appreciated.

5. Satterthwaite 2007: 1.

6. Lee 2007: 7.

7. Satterthwaite 2007: 29–30.

8. United Nations 2006.

9. Satterthwaite 2007: 29.

10. Wright 2002: 72–3.

11. McMichael 2000.

12. UNDP 2005.

13. McMichael 2000.

14. Sutcliffe 2001.

15. The global city thesis suggests that cities are positioned in highly

differentiated points in a broader global hierarchy of cities. This 'hierarchy' holds determining implications for the capacity of the city to engage with and survive the new economic processes that rode on the wave technological advances that made extended trade and exchange flows possible. For instance, the top tier in the hierarchy would be dominated by London, Tokyo and New York; the second level will hold cities of regional importance, e.g. Amsterdam, Frankfurt and Los Angeles; the third tier would reflect significant internationally recognized capitals such as Madrid and Sydney; the fourth level would reflect cities of national importance and some international functions, e.g. Milan and Osaka. In other words, in terms of the logic of the global economy, this is a hierarchy based on the level of strategic importance for international capital. See Sassen 1994.

16. For a useful review, see UN–Habitat 2001: ch. 2.
17. Graham 2000: 183–4.
18. Graham 2000: 183–4.
19. Graham 2000: 185.
20. Graham 2000: 186.
21. For an insightful elaboration with examples of this point, see Graham and Marvin 2002: ch. 3.
22. The data for Table 2.3 come from Swilling 2006. The summarized descriptions provided by the knowledge-management company that developed the instrument deserve a discussion in their own right. It may interest the reader that Mark Swilling uses these data to calculate and demonstrate the differential contribution of wealthy and poor residents to the extraordinarily large ecological footprint of Cape Town.
23. The motor vehicle industry is the world's largest manufacturing business. In 2002 it was estimated that there were 600 million vehicles in the world and approximately 53 million were sold annually. It is anticipated that 66 per cent of sales growth over the next decade will come from the Asia-Pacific region, mainly China and India. See Gabel and Bruner 2003: 36–7.
24. Graham and Marvin 2001: 117.
25. This history is usefully set out in Zetter 2004.
26. Ya and Weliwita 2007: 4–5.
27. Tannerfeldt and Ljung 2006: 54.
28. Moreno and Warah 2006.
29. UN–Habitat 2006: 190.
30. Moreno and Warah 2006.
31. See Clarke 2006; de Souza 2005; Standing 2004.
32. Neuwirth 2005.
33. Lee 2007: 16 (see this reference for original source).
34. Tibaijuka 2005: 18–19.
35. Moreno and Warah 2006.
36. Tibaijuka 2005: 19.

Chapter 3

1. UN–Habitat 2004a: 14.
2. UN–Habitat 2004a: 21–2.
3. UN–Habitat 2004a: 25.
4. UN–Habitat 2004a: 64–5.
5. Press release, 'United Nations Expert on Adequate Housing Concludes Visit to South Africa', www.ohchr.org; accessed 28 November 2007.
6. UN–Habitat 2004a: 32.
7. UN–Habitat 2004a: 33–4.
8. De Soto 2000. I will return to de Soto's influence later on in the chapter.
9. UN–Habitat 2004a: 32.
10. Lee 2007.
11. UN–Habitat 2004a: 39; see also UN–Habitat 2004b for a range of examples that can be linked to each of these tenure forms.
12. Fernandez 2002: 5–8.
13. De Soto 2005.
14. Smolka and Larangeira 2007.
15. Smolka and Laraggeira 2007.
16. Fernandez 2002: 7.
17. Fernandez 2002: 7.
18. UN–Habitat 2004a: esp. 35.
19. UN–Habitat 2004a: 36. Also see a recent piece by one of the leading policy minds in UN–Habitat on the importance of the rental route in relation to the massive market failure, evidenced most clearly in the sheer absence of financing instruments tailored to the realities of the urban poor: You 2007.
20. UN–Habitat 2004a: 37.
21. South Africa is an interesting example of likely private-sector behaviour because the financial services sector is matured, there is a willingness on the part of the state to underwrite such transactions, and the banks are compelled by an industry charter to develop products for the lower ends of the market. Nevertheless, up until now the dominant trend is market avoidance.
22. UN–Habitat 2004a: 41.
23. For a fascinating and counter-intuitive exploration of these issues and their implications for economic development, see Benjamin 2004.
24. Riddell 2004.
25. A particularly instructive case is the dramatic progress Bogota has made in just over a decade to expand dramatically access for the urban poor (and non-poor) to crucial public infrastructures such as transport, cycle lanes, parks and, most impressively, well-designed and well-stocked libraries that are interlaced with the transport and public space systems (see e.g. Cabbalero 2003; Wright and Montezuma 2004).
26. It is crucial to recognize that the task force did not simply accept target

11 because it was regarded as too limited and instead introduced the following formulation: 'By 2020, improving substantially the lives of at least 100 million slum dwellers, while providing adequate alternatives to new slum formation.' This is highly significant because the growth of slums is projected to be well above 100 million people. So, in effect the document seeks to make a much more substantial intervention than what the original target established. See: UN Millennium Project 2005: 3. However, here I am not delving into the overarching argument of the document, which is very strong, but rather focus on the approach to civil society participation.

27. In particular, see UN–Habitat 2004a: 60 para. 2.
28. My perspective is informed by a study Firoz Khan and I conducted of the growth and institutional dynamics of the South African Homeless People's Federation. See Khan and Pieterse 2006.
29. UN–Habitat 2004a: 58.
30. UN–Habitat 2003: xxvii.
31. Swilling 2006. The list of proposals that follow are all adapted from this same source.
32. Swilling 2006: 48.

Chapter 4

1. A useful review of these trends can be found in Manor 1999.
2. Habitat 1996.
3. UN–Habitat 2002: 15.
4. UN–Habitat 2002: 15.
5. UN–Habitat 2002: 16.
6. See the review of Manor 2004.
7. For more explicit elaborations of this phenomenon, see Cornwall 2004; Miraftab 2004, etc. For a more nuanced articulation of this argument, see Williams 2004.
8. UN–Habitat 2002: 11.
9. Mumtaz and Wegelin 2001: 126.
10. Pieterse 2000.
11. Dialogical is derived from dialogue, which in turn can mean discussion, exchange of ideas, flow of information, and so forth. Theoretically, dialogical draws on the work of Jürgen Habermas on communicative action to democratize the public sphere (see Healey 1997 for a creative adaptation of Habermas's theories to urban politics and planning; and Flyvbjerg 1998 for a systematic critique).
12. Borja and Castells 1997: 154.
13. Cities Alliance website: www.citiesalliance.org; accessed 26 October 2007.
14. See World Bank 2000: 64.
15. Cities Alliance 2001: 1.

16. Cities Alliance 2001: 1.
17. Cities Alliance 2006. This document systematizes the lessons from practical experiences in undertaking CDSs and responding to new development priorities such as climate change and associated environmental risks.
18. Cities Alliance 2006: 42.
19. Cities Alliance 2006: 3. Each of these themes is further subdivided in sub-themes which are also of great importance.
20. I am assuming here that most local governments in cities of the global South are democratically elected. Obviously my analysis does not apply in the same way where this is still not the case.
21. Cities Alliance 2006: 42.
22. Borja and Castells 1997: 154, 155.
23. Healey 1997: 284.
24. Healey 2000: 526.
25. Landry 2000.
26. Cities Alliance 2006: 4.
27. Graham and Marvin 2001.
28. UN–Habitat 2001.
29. UN–Habitat 2001: 26.
30. UN–Habitat 2001: 30.
31. Cities Alliance 2006: 33.
32. This figure is an adaptation of a model developed by Stephen Boshoff, the former chief city planner of the City of Cape Town municipality.

Chapter 5

1. Okri 1997: 32.
2. Simons 1995: 3.
3. In urban studies the actor-network approach of Ash Amin and Nigel Thrift (2002) stands out along with the post-Marxist formulation of Kian Tajbakhsh (2001). In development studies, Norman Long (2001) has gone a long way in formulating a sophisticated framework to capture the dynamic interplay between structure and agency and the space for political action beyond the restrictions of economic-deterministic epistemologies. These are consistent with scholarship in postcolonial cultural studies (Ahluwalia 2001; Ashcroft 2001).
4. See Amin and Thrift 2002: ch 6.
5. Two scholars who are particularly insightful on this point are de Sousa Santos 1995; Unger 1998.
6. For example, see Gabardi 2001; Mouffe 2000; Squires 2002.
7. See Flood 1999.
8. Healey 2000: 918.
9. In other words, it is related to, but more narrow than, the Foucauldian conception, whereby 'Government is any more or less calculated and rational activity, undertaken by a multiplicity of authorities and agencies, employing a variety of techniques and forms of knowledge, that seeks to

shape conduct by working through our desires, aspirations, interests and beliefs, for definite but shifting ends and with a diverse set of relatively unpredictable consequences, effects and outcomes' (Dean 1999: 11).

10. Gabardi 2001: 82.
11. Healey 2000: 919.
12. The rich and insightful work of Doreen Massey 1999 is particularly illuminating on this point.
13. Tajbakhsh 2001: 6.
14. Cleaver 2001: 44.
15. Cleaver 2001: 44.
16. Flyvbjerg 2001: ch. 8; Gabardi 2001: ch. 4.
17. Goetz and Lister 2001; Heller 2001.
18. In an earlier study I provide a full discussion on the gamut of participatory governance policies and tools with due regard for contextual specificity and dangers associated with this relatively recent trend: Pieterse 2000. Also see Borja and Castells 1997: 193–200; Goetz and Gaventa 2001; Manor 2004.
19. See Barkin 1997; Mossberger and Stoker 2001.
20. See UN–Habitat's own experience and research in this regard: Lüdeking and Williams 1999.
21. Borja and Castells 1997.
22. See Shubane 1995.
23. For example, see Bond 2000.
24. There is a rich literature on this which provides useful guidelines for thinking through the complex relational politics; see especially Edmunds and Wollenberg 2001; Hillier 2002.
25. There are obviously many instances where (relatively) privileged and conservative groups also embark on direct action to get their political grievances across. By focusing on disadvantaged groups I am merely signalling an analytical preference to highlight the actions of this category of social actors but not to create an impression that other groups do not engage in this political arena.
26. Alvarez et al. 1998; Orbach 1996.
27. Scott 1997: 323.
28. This is surveyed in Pieterse 2001.
29. Appadurai 2004: 69.
30. Evans 2002.
31. This is not to denigrate the important and complex work of effective institutional change in large public-sector organizations. Studies on 'synergy' between the state and civil society organizations demonstrate just how crucial it is to pursue organizational transformation to enhance the developmental capability of government departments, especially where they act in concert with civil society organizations (see Evans 1996; Tendler 1997; Abers 2000). Nevertheless, drawing on participant observations, I am also certain that much of what passes as change-

management quickly becomes ritualized practices of adaptation with little interest in fulfilling the developmental mandate of the government.
32. Barnard and Armstrong 1998.
33. See Bauman and Mitlin 2002.
34. Goverde et al. 2000: 14.
35. Gabardi 2001: 89.
36. Robinson 2002.
37. See Graham and Marvin 2001.
38. The theoretical basis of such an approach is elaborated in: Eade and Mele 2002; Massey 1999; Robinson 2002; and Tajbakhsh 2001. Strategic actions that flow from such an approach are deftly argued in Amin 2002; Amin and Thrift 2002; Graham and Marvin 2001: Postscript; and Sorkin 2001.
39. Bayat 1997, 2000; Scott 1997.
40. Bayat 2000: 24–5.
41. Barker 2000: 151.
42. Gabardi 2001: 109.
43. Amin and Thrift 2002: ch. 6; Mouffe 2000.
44. Holston 1998.

Chapter 6

1. Cities Alliance 2006: 17.
2. Healey 2000a.
3. Coates (2003: 17) explains that Ecstacity is 'an imaginary place that foregrounds the sensual side of all cities. To help construct it, I have taken fragments from seven cities around the world, and woven them into one multi-coloured urban fabric. Its patterns shift according to the overlap of cultures. It both reconfigures what we already know and stimulates new responses.'
4. For example, see Eade and Mele 2002; Tajbakhsh 2001.
5. Rakodi and Lloyd-Jones 2002.
6. Coates 2003: 43.
7. Bayat 1997: 8.
8. Bayat 1997: 10–11.
9. This section draws on a previously published chapter: Khan and Pieterse 2006.
10. People's Dialogue 1996: 21.
11. People's Dialogue 1996: 21; 2000.
12. People's Dialogue 1996: 21.
13. J. Bolnick, interview, 7 April 2004, Cape Town.
14. Shack/Slum Dwellers International (SDI), a global network of poor people's organizations from eleven countries of the South, comprises federations of community organizations that are linked to NGOs and groupings of professionals who support federation initiatives. Unlike other transnational citizen networks, the locus of power lies in communities themselves rather than in intermediary NGOs at national and

international levels. This is partly because the SDI and its counterparts were not set up to influence global policymaking or lobby international financial institutions (though these roles are increasing). Rather, their aim is to promote practical solidarity, mutual support and the exchange of information about strategies and concrete alternatives among their members (Edwards 2001).

15. Development Works 2003.
16. The United Nation's Commission for Human Settlements (UNCHS) and the United Nations Development Programme (UNDP) – co-convenors of the Habitat II Conference – and the United States Agency for International Development.
17. Huchzermeyer 2001: 322.
18. Huchzermeyer 2001: 323.
19. See www.sdinet.org/documents/doc16.htm, accessed 19 November 2007.
20. Personal correspondence with the Mark Swilling based on assessment of SDI he carried out in East Africa 2006.
21. The sources for the textbox are Brillembourg and Klumpner 2005: 19; and www.u-tt.com, accessed 30 July 2007.
22. Ferrándiz 2004.
23. Rodgers 2004.
24. Standing 2004.
25. Clarke 2006.
26. Winton 2004.
27. See de Sousa 2005; Winton 2004; Zaluar 2006.
28. De Sousa 2005: 6–7.
29. Neate and Platt 2006: 102.
30. Research by various scholars indicates that during the past two decades, in tandem with intensifying globalization processes, the scale, complexity and reach of drug economies (and markets) have exploded, leaving a devastating legacy of crime and violence in their wake (Castells 1997; Naím 2006). During this same period economic contraction and restructuring (to more service-based sectors, which require higher skill levels) has tended to worsen income inequalities in most cities, leaving the most marginalized in even more precarious situations with little hope of incorporation into the formal labour market (UNDP 1998). As a consequence of these forces, many black youths, especially men, are enrolled in one form or another into gangs that manage and drive, in particular the drug trade in poor neighbourhoods. Poor neighbourhoods fulfil particular functions in an extensive and often globalized value chain of production, refinement, manufacturing, warehousing, distribution and consumption in local, national and global markets. Around these activities, drug-based gangs exercise near total control of the territories where they are located, often in collusion with elements in the security forces (de Souza 2005).
31. For a fascinating reading of the significance of this group, see Caldeira 2004.

32. MV Bill quoted in Neate 2003: 191–2. MV Bill (Alexandre Barreto) is a hip-hop artist from one of the most violent regions of the city of Rio de Janeiro, the *favela* of Cidade de Deus (City of God).
33. From an interview in *Leros Magazine*, June 2005, www.leros.co.uk; accessed 21 October 2006.
34. Pardue 2004.
35. Interview with Luis Soares, www.dreamscanbe.org/controlPanel/materia/view/433; accessed 21 October 2006.
36. Sarai Collective, 'Sarai: The New Media Initiative' http://subsol.c3.hu/subsol_2/contributorso/saraitext.html; accessed 8 November 2007.
37. Ibid.
38. Ibid.
39. www.sarai.net/about-us/introducing-sarai/overview; accessed 8 November 2007.
40. www.chimurenga.co.za/html; accessed 8 November 2007.
41. This crude summary of the important work of *Chimurenga* cannot substitute for exploring this initiative first hand by visiting their website and buying their wares.

Chapter 7

1. Habitat 1996: para. 29.
2. NSFWUS 2000: 7.
3. NSFWUS 2000: 8.
4. Human rights, www.reference.com/browse/wiki/Human_rights; accessed 5 November 2007.
5. There is another layer to the issue of a comprehensive approach to rights, which is the importance of adopting a multicultural lens to view the question of rights and their localization in particular regions and countries. This argument has been fruitfully expounded by Bouventura de Sousa Santos (1999).
6. This section draws on, and is more fully developed in, another publication: Parnell and Pieterse 2007.
7. See Friedmann 2002: ch. 4, for a similar kind of argument but through the lens of 'insurgent citizenship'.
8. Florida 2005.
9. Robinson and Tinker 1998: 25.
10. For example, a leading business magazine, *Strategy and Business*, carried an article in which the following case was made: 'The quality of infrastructure and land-use planning "hard wires" the environmental impact of a given region. The more consciously we can build infrastructure that doesn't harm, or that even helps restore, the natural environment, the more likely it is that those cities will endure' (Finn and Rahl 2007: 50).
11. See Walsh 2007; Doerr 2006.
12. Parnell 2007.
13. Riddel 2004: 258–60.

14. Young 2000: 206, 207.
15. Savage et al. 2003.
16. See Stevenson 2003; Tajbakhsh 2001.
17. Bridge and Watson 2000: 253.
18. Eade and Mele 2002.
19. Stevenson 2003: 40.
20. Tajbakhsh 2001: 28.
21. Smith 2001.
22. Clifford 2000; Massey 1999.
23. Stevenson 2003: 47.
24. Bridge and Watson 2000: 257–9; Marcuse 2000.
25. Bridge and Watson 2000: 257.
26. The points in this section draw on Healey's subtle and insightful framework on the dimensions of governance (see Table 1.1).
27. This section draws on an argument elaborated more fully elsewhere: Pieterse 2006.
28. For an elaboration, see Barker 2000.
29. Gunder 2003: 253.
30. Ashcroft and Alhuwalia 1999: 135; the closing words are from Edward Said.
31. Cornell West, quoted in Ashcroft 2001: 49.
32. I am indebted to Ahmedi Vawda for the reminder that what is considered 'radical' and 'establishment' is profoundly generational. Youth always carries within itself very particular ideas about what is radical and cutting-edge, as changing fashions in popular culture and politics remind us.
33. I believe that a number of epistemic communities need to coexist and will do in practice. However, for the sake of the argument in the book, I hereon refer to epistemic community in the singular because I am invoking one that I can identify with.
34. I am fully aware that a number of objections to the notion of an epistemic community or organic intellectuals can be raised but refer the reader to another source where I have dealt with those: Pieterse 2006.
35. Brenner and Theodore 2002.
36. See Fernandes 2007; Ministry of Cities 2005.
37. This avenue of area-based planning has attracted a lot of scholarly criticism; see for example Miraftab 2007.
38. See Appadurai 2002; Swilling 2006, on such counter-governmentalities in the practices of Shack/Slum Dwellers International.
39. Scott et al. 2002.
40. Healey 2007.
41. Barton et al. 2003: 1.

Chapter 8

1. Sallis 2000: 13–14.
2. See: Parnell and Pieterse 1999: 7.

3. The general structural causes of poverty at a global scale are clearly and aptly summarized by Christian Aid: 'Poverty is caused by unequal power relations within and amongst countries. Structural causes of poverty ensure an adverse redistribution from the poor to the rich: the debt service burden, unfair terms of trade and trade rules that favour rich companies based in the North, and the lack of resources for investment. Market incentives ensure that the benefits of technology and globalization accrue to the rich. Present systems of governance are ill-equipped to address these causes; there are no accountability systems to regulate transnational corporations and only imperfect accountability for the IMF, the World Bank and the WTO. Amongst attempted solutions, economic growth has enjoyed the greatest support. But even "pro-poor" growth has failed to overcome poverty, because it does not challenge the unequal distribution of resources. In fact, macroeconomic reform and fiscal stringency have required governments to withdraw resources from poor people' (quoted in Christie and Warburton 2001: 114).
4. See Pieterse 2001 for the sources that inform this typology.
5. Fowler 1997.
6. For a fuller review of these debates, see Pieterse 2001.
7. Pieterse and van Donk 2002.
8. Part of the problem of the left has been its ambivalence towards institutions, if not downrights dismissal of them because the codification that accompanies institutionalization tends to encrust new lines of inclusion/exclusion. This is not the place to explore this theme in any great depth but I do think that the fear of contamination that invariably accompanies institutionalization is an important part of why progressives are often so short on implementable alternatives with regard to urban policy.
9. Total autonomy or independence is, of course, highly unlikely and improbable, especially since former anti-colonial movements are often today part of the ruling elite in democracies of the South. As a consequence, these movements/parties remain hugely influential in shaping the dynamics within civil society.
10. The organizational sensibility I have in mind here is analogous to the critical praxis that arises from Freierean critical pedagogy, which in turn can be extended to the politics of decolonizing interiority of Frantz Fanon and Steve Biko. The evocative theorizations of organizational development scholar Alan Kaplan (2000) come to mind.
11. See van Donk et al. 2008; Harrison et al. 2003.
12. For example, see Fernandes 2007.
13. Pieterse 2006.

References

Abers, R. (2000) *Inventing Local Democracy: Grassroots Politics in Brazil*, Boulder CO and London: Lynne Rienner.

Ahluwalia, P. (2001) *Politics and Post-Colonial Theory: African Inflections*, London: Routledge.

Alvarez, S., Dagnino, E., and Escobar, A. (1998) 'Introduction: The Cultural and the Political in Latin American Social Movements', in S. Alvarez, E. Dagnino and A. Escobar (eds), *Cultures of Politics, Politics of Cultures: Re-visioning Latin American Social Movements*, Boulder CO and Oxford: Westview Press.

Amin, A. (2002) 'Ethnicity and the Multicultural City', *Environment and Planning* 34(6): 959–80.

Amin, A. (2006) 'The Good City', *Urban Studies* 43(5/6): 1009–23.

Amin, A., and Thrift, N. (2002) *Cities: Reimagining the Urban*, Cambridge: Polity Press.

Amin, A., and Thrift, N. (2005) 'What is Left? Only the Future', *Antipode* 37(2): 220–38.

Andersson, G. (1999) 'Partnerships between CBOs, NGOs and Government in South Africa: Insights Derived from Experience', Pretoria: USAID South Africa.

Appadurai, A. (2002) 'Deep Democracy: Urban Governmentality and the Horizon of Politics', *Public Culture* 14(1): 21–47.

Appadurai, A. (2004) 'The Capacity to Aspire: Culture and the Terms of Recognition', in V. Rao and M. Walton (eds), *Culture and Public Action*, Stanford CA: Stanford University Press.

Ashcroft, B. (2001) *Post-Colonial Transformations*, London: Routledge.

Ashcroft, B., and Ahulwalia, P. (1999) *Edward Said: The Paradox of Identity*, London: Routledge.

Atkinson, A. (2004) 'Urbanization in a Neoliberal World – Exploring Escape Routes', *City* 8(1): 89–108.

Atkinson, A. (2005) 'Urban Development: Reviving and Activating Utopian Strategies', *City* 9(3): 279–95.

Barker, C. (2000) *Cultural Studies: Theory and Practice*, London: Sage.

Barkin, D. (1997) 'Will Higher Productivity Improve Living Standards?', in R. Burgess, M. Carmona and T. Kolstee (eds), *The Challenge of Sustainable Cities: Neoliberalism and Urban Strategies in Developing Countries*, London: Zed Books.

Barnard, A., and Armstrong, G. (1998) 'Learning and Policy Integration', in J. Schnurr and S. Holtz (eds), *The Cornerstone of Development: Integrating Environmental, Social and Economic Policies*. Boca Raton: Lewis Publishers and IDRC.

Barnett, C. (2005) 'Consolations of Neoliberalism', *Geoforum* 36(1): 7–12.

Barton, H., Grant, M., and Guise, R. (2003) *Shaping Neighbourhoods: A Guide for Health, Sustainability and Vitality*, London and New York: Spon Press.

Bauman, T., and Mitlin, D. (2002) 'The South African Homeless Federation: Investing in the Poor', paper presented at Rural and Urban Development conference, Rietvleidam: History Workshop and National Land Committee.

Bayat, A. (1997) *Street Politics: Poor People's Movements in Iran*, New York: Columbia University Press.

Bayat, A. (2000) 'Social Movements, Activism and Social Development in the Middle East' *Civil Society and Social Movements Programme Paper*, Geneva: UNRISD.

Benjamin, S. (2004) 'Urban Land Transformation for Pro-poor Economies', *Geoforum* 35(2): 177–87.

Bond, P. (2000) *Elite Transition: From Apartheid to Neoliberalism in South Africa*, London and Pietermaritzburg: Pluto and University of Natal Press.

Borja, J., and Castells, M. (1997) *Local and Global: The Management of Cities in the Information Age*, London: Earthscan.

Brenner, N., and Theodore, N. (2002) 'Cities and the Geographies of "Actually Existing Neoliberalism"', *Antipode* 34(3): 349–79.

Bridge, G., and Watson, S. (2000) 'City Differences', in G. Bridge and S. Watson (eds), *A Companion to the City*, Oxford: Blackwell.

Brillembourg, A., and Klumpner, H. (2005) 'Introduction', in A. Brilembourg, K. Feireiss and H. Klumpner (eds), *Informal City: Caracas Case*, London: Prestel.

Byrne, D. (2001) *Understanding the Urban*, New York: Palgrave.

Cabbalero, M.C. (2003) *Biblored: Colombia's Innovative Library Network*. Washington DC: Council on Library and Information Resources.

Caldeira, T.P.R. (2004) 'Hip-Hop, Periphery, and Spatial Segregation in São

Paulo', paper presented at the symposium 'Urban Traumas: The City and Disasters', Center of Contemporary Culture of Barcelona, 7–11 July.

Calvino, I. (1997) *Invisible Cities*, London: Vintage.

Castells, M. (1997) *The Power of Identity*, vol. II of *The Information Age: Economy, Society, and Culture*, Oxford: Blackwell.

Christie, I., and Warburton, D. (2001) *From Here to Sustainability: Politics in the Real World*, London: Earthscan.

Cities Alliance (2001) 'City Development Strategies: The Cities Alliance Perspective', draft for discussion, Washington DC: Cities Alliance, www. citiesalliance.org; accessed 23 October 2007.

Cities Alliance (2006) *Guide to City Development Strategies: Improving Urban Performance*. Washington DC: Cities Alliance.

Clarke, C. (2006) 'Politics, Violence and Drugs in Kingston, Jamaica', *Bulletin of Latin American Research* 25(3): 420–40.

Cleaver, F. (2001) 'Institutions, Agency and the Limitations of Participatory Approaches to Development', in B. Cooke and U. Kothari (eds), *Participation: The New Tyranny?* London: Zed Books.

Clifford, J. (2000) 'Taking Identity Politics Seriously: "The Contradictory Stony Ground…"', in P. Gilroy, L. Grossberg and A. McRobbie (eds), *Without Guarantees: In Honour of Stuart Hall*. London: Verso.

Coates, N. (2003) *Guide to Ecstacity*, London: Laurence King.

Cornwall, A. (2004) 'Spaces for Transformation? Reflections on Issues of Power and Difference in Participation in Development', in S. Hickey and G. Mohan (eds), *Participation: From Tyranny to Transformation. Exploring New Approaches to Participation in Development*, London: Zed Books.

Cornwall, A., and Brock, K. (2005) 'What Do Buzzwords Do for Development Policy? A Critical Look at "Participation", "Empowerment" and "Poverty Reduction"', *Third World Quarterly* 26(7): 1043–60.

Davis, M. (2005) *Planet of Slums*, London: Verso.

de Boeck, P., and Plissart, M. (2004) *Kinshasa: Tales of the Invisible City*, Brussels: Ludion.

de Soto, H. (2000) *The Mystery of Capital*, New York: Basic Books.

de Soto, H. (2005) 'The Challenge of Connecting Informal and Formal Property Systems: Some Reflections Based on the Case of Tanzania', Lima: Instituto Libertad y Democracia.

de Sousa Santos, B. (1995) *Towards a New Common Sense: Law, Science and Politics in the Pragmatic Transition*, London: Routledge.

de Sousa Santos, B. (1999) 'Towards a Multicultural Conception of Human Rights', in M. Featherstone and S. Lash (eds), *Spaces of Culture: City – Nation – World*, London: Sage.

de Souza, M.L. (2005) 'Urban Planning in an Age of Fear: The Case of Rio de Janeiro', *International Development Planning Review* 27(1): 1–19.

Dean, M. (1999) *Governmentality: Power and Rule in Modern Society*, London: Sage.

Desai, A. (2000) *The Poors of Chatsworth: Race, Class and Social Movements in Post-Apartheid South Africa*, Durban: Madiba.

Development Works (2003) 'Cities Alliance Project on a Pro-Poor Slum Upgrading Framework for South Africa for Submission to the Cities Alliance/United Nations Centre for Human Settlements', report for People's Dialogue, Johannesburg.

Doerr, J. (2006) 'California's Global-Warming Solution', *Time*, 3 September, www.time.com/time/magazine/article/0,9171,1531324,00.html; accessed 30 November 2007.

Duiker, S. (2000) *Thirteen Cents*, Cape Town: David Philip.

Eade, J., and Mele, C. (2002) 'Introduction: Understanding the City', in J. Eade and C. Mele (eds), *Understanding the City: Contemporary and Future Perspectives*, Oxford: Blackwell.

Edmunds, D., and Wollenberg, E. (2001) 'A Strategic Approach to Multi-stakeholder Negotiations', *Development and Change* 32(2): 231–53.

Edwards, M. (2001) 'Global Civil Society and Community Exchanges: A Different Form of Movement', *Environment and Urbanisation* 13(2): 145–9.

Evans, P. (1996) 'Introduction: Development Strategies across the Public–Private Divide', *World Development* 24(6): 1033–37.

Evans, P. (2002) 'Introduction: Looking for Agents of Urban Liveability in a Globalized Political Economy', in P. Evans (ed.), *Livable Cities? Urban Struggles for Livelihood and Sustainability*, Berkeley: University of California Press.

Fernandez, E. (2002) 'The Influence of de Soto's *The Mystery of Capital*', *Land Lines*, January: 5–8.

Fernandez, E. (2007) 'Land Governance and Popular Participation in Urban Management. Possibilities and Limitations of Socio-spatial and Political Inclusion in Brazil', paper presented at Western Cape Integrated Development Planning Annual Conference, Cape Town, May.

Ferrándiz, F. (2004) 'The Body as Wound: Possession, Malandros and Everyday Violence in Venezuela', *Critique of Anthropology* 24(2): 107–33.

Finn, M., and Rahl, G. (2007) 'The Environment: Let's Get It Right', *Strategy & Business* 47: 46.

Flood, R.L. (1999) *Rethinking the Fifth Discipline: Learning within the Unknowable*, London and New York: Routledge.

Florida, R. (2005) *Cities and the Creative Class*, New York and London: Routledge.

Flyvbjerg, B. (1998) 'Empowering Civil Society: Habermas, Foucault and the Question of Conflict', in M. Douglas and J. Friedmann (eds), *Cities for Citizens: Planning and the Rise of Civil Society in a Global Age*, Chichester: John Wiley.

Flyvbjerg, B. (2001) *Making Social Science Matter: Why Social Inquiry Fails and How it Can Count Again*, London: Sage.

Flyvbjerg, B. (2004) 'Phronetic Planning Research: Theoretical and Methodological Reflections', *Planning Theory and Practice* 5(3): 283–306.

Fowler, A. (1997) *Striking a Balance: A Guide to Enhancing the Effectiveness of Non-governmental Organisations in International Development*, London: Earthscan.

Friedmann, J. (2002) *The Prospect of Cities*, Minneapolis and London: University of Minnesota Press.

Fung, A., and Wright, E.O. (2001) 'Deepening Democracy: Innovations in Empowered Participatory Governance', *Politics and Society* 29(1): 5–41.

Gabardi, W. (2001) *Negotiating Postmodernism*, Minneapolis: University of Minnesota Press.

Gabel, M., and Bruner, H. (2003) *Global Inc. An Atlas of the Multinational Corporation*, New York: New Press.

Goetz, A., and Gaventa, J. (2001) 'From Consultation to Influence: Bringing Citizen Voice and Client Focus into Service Delivery', *IDS Working Paper* no. 138, Brighton: Institute for Development Studies.

Goetz, A.M., and Lister, S. (2001) 'The Politics of Civil Society Engagement with the State: A Comparative Analysis of South Africa and Uganda', Brighton: Institute of Development Studies.

Goverde, H., Cerny, P.G., Haugaard, M., and Lentner, H. (2000) 'General Introduction: Power in Contemporary Politics', in H. Goverde, P.G. Cerny, M. Haugaard and H. Lentner (eds), *Power in Contemporary Politics: Theories, Practices, Globalizations*, London: Sage.

Graham, S. (2000) 'Constructing Premium Network Spaces: Reflections on Infrastructure Networks and Contemporary Urban Development', *International Journal of Urban and Regional Research* 24(1): 183–4.

Graham, S., and Marvin, S. (2001) *Splintering Urbanism: Networked Infrastructures, Technological Mobilities and the Urban Condition*, London and New York: Routledge.

Gunder, M. (2003) 'Passionate Planning for the Other's Desire: An Agonistic Response to the Dark Side of Planning', *Progress in Planning* 60(3): 235–319.

Habitat (United Nations Centre for Human Settlements) (1996) *The Habitat Agenda*, Nairobi: Habitat.

Hall, S. (1996) 'When Was "The Post-Colonial"? Thinking at the Limit', in I. Chambers and L. Curti (eds), *The Postcolonial Question: Common Skies, Divided Horizons*, London: Routledge.

Harrison, P., Huchzermeyer, M., and Mayekiso, M. (eds) (2003) *Confronting Fragmentation: Housing and Urban Development in a Democratising Society*, Cape Town: UCT Press.

Harvey, D. (2006) *Space of Global Capitalism: Towards a Theory of Uneven Geographical Development*, London: Verso.

Healey, P. (1997) *Collaborative Planning: Shaping Places in Fragmented Societies*, London: Macmillan.

Healey, P. (2000a) 'Planning in Relational Space and Time: Responding to New Urban Realities', in G. Bridge and S. Watson (eds), *A Companion to the City*, Oxford: Blackwell.

Healey, P. (2000b) 'Planning Theory and Urban and Regional Dynamics:

A Comment on Yiftachel and Huxley', *International Journal of Urban and Regional Research* 24(4): 917–21.

Healey, P. (2002) 'On Creating the "City" as a Collective Resource', *Urban Studies* 39(10): 1777–92.

Healey, P. (2004) 'Creativity and Urban Governance', *Policy Studies* 25(2): 87–102.

Healey, P. (2007) *Urban Complexity and Spatial Strategies: Towards a Relational Planning for Our Times*, London: Routledge.

Heller, P. (2001) 'Moving the State: The Politics of Democratic Decentralization in Kerala, South Africa, and Porto Alegre', *Politics and Society* 29(1): 131–63.

Hillier, J. (2002) 'Direct Action and Agonism in Democratic Planning Processes', in P. Allmendinger and M. Twedwr-Jones (eds), *Planning Futures: New Directions for Planning Theory*, London: Routledge.

Holston, J. (1998) 'Spaces of Insurgent Citizenship', in L. Sandercock (ed.), *Making the Invisible Visible: A Multicultural Planning History*, Berkeley: University of California Press.

Huchzermeyer, M. (2001) 'Housing for the Poor: Negotiated Housing Policy in South Africa', *Habitat International* 25: 303–31.

Jack, M. (2006) 'Urbanisation, Sustainable Growth and Poverty Reduction in Asia', *IDS Bulletin* 37(3): 101–14.

Kaplan, A. (2002) *Development Practitioners and Social Process: Artists of the Invisible*, London: Pluto.

Khan, F., and Pieterse, E. (2006) 'The Homeless People's Alliance: Purposive Creation and Ambiguated Realities', in R. Ballard, A. Habib and I. Valodia (eds), *Voices of Protest: Social Movements in Post-Apartheid South Africa*, Pietermaritzburg: University of KwaZulu–Natal Press.

Landry, C. (2000) *The Creative City: A Toolkit for Urban Innovators*, London: Comedia and Earthscan.

Lee, K.N. (2007) 'An Urbanizing World', in L. Starke (ed.), *State of the World 2007: Our Urban Future*, New York and London: W.W. Norton.

Lingis, A. (1994) *Abuses*, Berkeley: University of California Press.

Lingis, A. (2004) *Dangerous Emotions*, Berkeley: University of California Press.

Long, N. (2001) *Development Sociology: Actor Perspectives*, London: Routledge.

Lüdeking, G., and Williams, C. (1999) 'Poverty, Participation and Government Enablement. A Summary of Findings, Lessons Learned and Recommendations of Habitat/ISS Evaluation Research (1996–1998)', Nairobi: Habitat.

Manor, J. (1999) *The Political Economic of Democratic Decentralization*, Washington DC: World Bank.

Manor, J. (2004) 'Democratisation with Inclusion: Political Reforms and People's Empowerment at the Grassroots', *Journal of Human Development* 5(1): 5–29.

Marcuse, P. (2000) 'Cities in Quarters', in G. Bridge and S. Watson (eds), *A Companion to the City*, Oxford: Blackwell.

Massey, D. (1999) 'Cities in the World', in D. Massey, J. Allen and S. Pile (eds), *City Worlds*, New York: Routledge.

McMichael, P. (2000) *Development and Social Change: A Global Perspective*, Thousand Oaks CA: Pine Forge Press.

Ministry of Cities (2005) *Land Regularization*, Brasilia: Ministry of Cities.

Miraftab, F. (2004) 'Making Neo-liberal Governance: The Disempowering Work of Empowerment', *International Planning Studies* 9(4): 239–59.

Miraftab, F. (2007) 'Governing Post Apartheid Spatiality: Implementing City Improvement Districts in Cape Town', *Antipode* 39(4): 602–26.

Moore, D. (1994) 'Optics of Engagement: Power, Positionality and African Studies', *Transition* 63: 121–7.

Moreno, E.L., and Warah, R. (2006) 'Urban and Slum Trends in the 21st Century', *UN Chronicle Online Edition* 2, www.un.org/Pubs/chronicle/2006/issue2/0206p24.htm; accessed 19 November 2007.

Mossberger, K., and Stoker, G. (2001) 'The Evolution of Urban Regime Theory: The Challenge of Conceptualisation', *Urban Affairs Review* 36(6): 810–35.

Mouffe, C. (2000) *The Democratic Paradox*, London and New York: Verso.

Mumtaz, B., and Wegelin, E. (2001) *Guiding Cities: The UNDP/UNCHS/World Bank Urban Management Programme*, Nairobi: UN–Habitat.

Naím, M. (2006) *Illicit: How Smugglers, Traffickers, and Copycats are Hijacking the Global Economy*, London: Heinemann.

Neate, P. (2003) *Where You're At: Notes from the Frontline of a Hip Hop Planet*, London: Bloomsbury.

Neate, P., and Platt, D. (2006) *Culture is Our Weapon: Afroreggae in the Favelas of Rio*, London: Latin American Bureau.

Nederveen Pieterse, J. (2001) 'Participatory Democracy Reconceived', *Futures* 33(5): 407–22.

Neuwirth, R. (2005) *Shadow Cities: A Billion Squatters, A New Urban World*, New York: Routledge.

NSFWUS (National Science Foundation Workshop on Urban Sustainability) (2000) 'Towards a Comprehensive Geographical Perspective on Urban Sustainability. Final Report of the 1998 National Science Foundation Workshop on Urban Sustainability', Rutgers University, New Jersey.

Okri, B. (1997) *A Way of Being Free*, London: Phoenix House.

Orbach, S. (1996) 'Couching Anxieties', in S. Dunant and R. Porter (eds), *The Age of Anxiety*, London: Virago.

Pardue, D. (2004) '"Writing in the Margins": Brazilian Hip-Hop as an Educational Project', *Anthropology and Education Quarterly* 34(4): 411–32.

Parnell, S. (2007) 'Urban Governance in the South: The Politics of Rights and Development', in K. Cox, M. Louw and J. Robinson (eds), *A Handbook of Political Geography*, London: Sage.

Parnell, S., and Pieterse, E. (1999) 'Municipal Poverty Reduction Framework: Technical Reports on Municipal Poverty Reduction Frameworks for the Cape Metropolitan Area', Cape Town: Isandla Institute.

Parnell, S., and Pieterse, E. (2007) Realising the "Right to the City":

Institutional Imperatives for Tackling Urban Poverty', paper presented to Living on the Margins Conference, Centre for Chronic Poverty, Plaas and Isandla Institute, Cape Town.

People's Dialogue (1996) 'What Are Those Bastards Up To Now? A Review of the Interactions between the South African Homeless People's Federation/People Dialogue Alliance and the South African Government of National Unity', www.dialogue.org.za/pd/bastards.htm.

People's Dialogue (2000) 'The Age of Cities and Organisations of the Urban Poor', unpublished mimeo (available from authors).

Pieterse, E. (2000) *Participatory Urban Governance: Practical Approaches, Regional Trends and UMP Experiences* 25, Nairobi: Urban Management Programme.

Pieterse, E. (2001) 'In Praise of Transgression: Notes on Institutional Synergy and Poverty Reduction', *Development Update* 3(4): 39–69.

Pieterse, E. (2004) 'Sketches of Development Praxis against a Horizon of Complexity', in E. Pieterse and F. Meintjies (eds), *Voices of the Transition: The Politics, Poetics and Practices of Development in South Africa*. Johannesburg: Heinemann.

Pieterse, E. (2005) 'Transgressing the Limits of Possibility: Working Notes on a Relational Model of Urban Politics', in A. Simone and A. Abouhani (eds), *Urban Processes and Change in Africa*, London: Zed Books.

Pieterse, E. (2006) 'Building with Ruins and Dreams: Exploratory Thoughts on Realising Integrated Urban Development through Crises', *Urban Studies* 43(2): 285–304.

Pieterse, E., and van Donk, M. (2002) 'Capacity Building for Poverty Reduction', *Dark Roast Occasional Paper* 8, Cape Town: Isandla Institute.

Rakodi, C., and Lloyd-Jones, T. (eds) (2002) *Urban Livelihoods: A People-Centred Approach to Reducing Poverty*, London: Earthscan.

Riddell, R. (2004) *Sustainable Urban Planning: Tipping the Balance*, Oxford: Blackwell.

Robinson, J. (2002) 'Global and World Cities: A View from Off the Map', *International Journal of Urban and Regional Research* 26(3): 531–54.

Robinson, J., and Tinker, J. (1998) 'Reconciling Ecological, Economic, and Social Imperatives', in J. Schnurr and S. Holtz (eds), *The Cornerstone of Development: Integrating Environmental, Social, and Economic Policies*, Ottawa and Boca Raton: IDRC and Lewis Publishers.

Rodgers, D. (2004) '"Disembedding" The City: Crime, Insecurity and the Spatial Organization of Managua, Nicaragua', *Environment and Urbanization* 16(2): 113–23.

Roe, E. (1993) 'Against Power: For the Politics of Complexity', *Transition* 62: 90–104.

Roy, A. (2005) 'Urban Informality: Towards an Epistemology of Planning', *Journal of the American Planning Association* 71(2): 147–58.

Roy, A., and Alsayyad, N. (eds) (2004) *Urban Informality: Transnational Perspectives from the Middle East, Latin America and South Asia*, Lanham MD: Lexington Books.

Sallis, J. (2000) *Gently into the Land of Meateaters*, Seattle: Black Heron Press.

Sandercock, L. (1998) 'The Death of Modernist Planning: Radical Praxis for a Postmodern Age', in M. Douglas and J. Friedmann (eds), *Cities for Citizens: Planning and the Rise of Civil Society in a Global Age*, Chichester: John Wiley.

Sassen, S. (1994) *Cities in a World Economy*, London: Pine Forge Press.

Satterthwaite, D. (2007) 'The Transition to a Predominantly Urban World and Its Underpinnings', Human Settlements Discussion Paper, London: International Institute for Environment and Development.

Savage, M., Warde, A., and Ward, K. (2003) *Urban Sociology, Capitalism and Modernity*, London: Palgrave Macmillan.

Scott, J.C. (1997) 'The Infrapolitics of Subordinate Groups', in M. Rahnema and V. Bawtree (eds), *The Post-Development Reader*, London: Zed Books.

Sharp, J., et al. (2000) 'Entanglements of Power: Geographies of Domination/Resistance', in J. Sharp, P. Routledge, C. Philo and R. Paddison (eds), *Entanglements of Power: Geographies of Domination/Resistance*, London: Routledge.

Shubane, K. (1995) 'Revisiting South African Conceptions of Civil Society', in R. Humpries and M. Reitzes (eds), *Civil Society after Apartheid*, Johannesburg: CPS and FES.

Simone, A. (2004) *For the City Yet to Come: Changing African Life in Four Cities*, Durham NC and London: Duke University Press.

Simons, J. (1995) *Foucault and the Political*, London and New York: Routledge.

Smith, M.P. (2001) *Transnational Urbanism: Locating Globalization*, Oxford: Blackwell.

Smolka, M., and Larangeira, A. (2007) 'Informality and Poverty in Latin American Urban Policies', unpublished paper.

Sorkin, M. (2001) *Some Assembly Required*, Minneapolis: University of Minnesota Press.

Soudien, C. (2003) 'Routes to Adulthood: Becoming a Young Adult in the New South Africa', *IDS Bulletin* 34(1): 63–71.

Squires, J. (2002) 'Democracy as Flawed Hegemon', *Economy and Society* 31(1): 132–51.

Standing, A. (2004) 'Out of the Mainstream: Critical Reflections on Organised Crime in the Western Cape', in B. Dixon and E. van der Spuy (eds), *Justice Gained? Crime and Crime Control in South Africa's Transition*, Cape Town: UCT Press.

Stevenson, D. (2003) *Cities and Urban Cultures*, Maidenhead: Open University Press.

Sutcliffe, B. (2001) *100 Ways of Seeing an Unequal World*, London: Zed Books.

Swilling, M. (2006) 'Sustainability and Infrastructure Planning in South Africa: A Cape Town Case Study', *Environment and Urbanization* 18(1): 23–50.

Swilling, M., and Russell, B. (2002) *The Size and Scope of the Non-profit Sector in South Africa*, Durban/Johannesburg: Center for Civil Society/Graduate School of Public and Development Management.

Tajbakhsh, K. (2001) *The Promise of the City: Space, Identity, and Politics in Contemporary Social Thought*, Berkeley: University of California Press.

Tannerfeldt, G., and Ljung, P. (2006) *More Urban Less Poor: An Introduction to Urban Development and Management,* London: Earthscan.

Tendler, J. (1997) *Good Government in the Tropics,* Baltimore and London: Johns Hopkins University Press.

Tibaijuka, A. (2005) 'Poverty and the Urban Agenda', *inFocus,* August: 18–19, Brasilia: UNDP International Poverty Centre.

UN Millennium Project (2005) *A Home in the City,* UN Millennium Task Force Report on Improving the Lives of Slums Dwellers, London: Earthscan.

UNDP (United Nations Development Programme) (1998) *Human Development Report 1998: Consumption for Human Development,* New York: UNDP.

UNDP (United Nations Development Programme) (2005) *Human Development Report 2005: International Cooperation at a Crossroads: Aid, Trade and Security in an Unequal World,* New York: UNDP.

UNFPA (United Nations Population Fund) (2007) *State of the World Population 2007,* New York: UNFPA.

Unger, R.M. (1998) *Democracy Realised: The Progressive Alternative,* London: Verso.

UN–Habitat (1996) *Istanbul Declaration,* Nairobi: United Nations Council for Human Settlements.

UN–Habitat (United Nations Human Settlements Programme) (2001) *Cities in a Globalizing World: Global Report on Human Settlements 2001,* London: Earthscan.

UN–Habitat (United Nations Human Settlement Programme) (2002) 'Global Campaign on Urban Governance. Concept Paper', Nairobi: UN–Habitat.

UN–Habitat (United Nations Human Settlements Programme) (2003) *The Challenge of Slums: Global Report on Human Settlements 2003,* London: Earthscan.

UN–Habitat (United Nations Human Settlements Programme) (2004a) *Global Campaign for Secure Tenure: A Tool for Advocating the Provision of Adequate Shelter for the Urban Poor,* concept paper, 2nd edn, Nairobi: UN–Habitat.

UN–Habitat (United Nations Human Settlements Programme) (2004b) *Land for All,* Nairobi: UN–Habitat.

UN–Habitat (United Nations Human Settlements Programme) (2006) *State of the World's Cities 2006/7: The Millennium Development Goals and Urban Sustainability.* London: Earthscan.

United Nations (2006) *World Urbanization Prospects: The 2005 Revision,* Fact Sheet 2: Urban Population in Major Urban Areas, Department of Economic and Social Affairs, Population Division.

van Donk, M., Swilling, M., Pieterse, E., and Parnell, S. (eds) (2008) *Consolidating Developmental Local Government: Lessons from the South Africa Experience,* Cape Town: UCT Press.

Walsh, B. (2007) 'California's Christmas List: Clean Air', *Time,* 8 November, www.time.com/time/printout/0,8816,1682116,00.html; accessed 30 November 2007.

Watson, V. (2006) 'Deep Difference: Diversity, Planning and Ethics', *Planning Theory* 5(1): 31–50.

Watson, V. (2007) 'Revisiting the Role of Urban Planning', concept paper pre-
pared for UN–Habitat for the 2009 Global Report on Human Settlements,
Cape Town: School of Architecture, Planning and Geomatics, University
of Cape Town.

Williams, G. (2004) 'Evaluating Participatory Development: Tyranny, Power
and (Re)politicisation', *Third World Quarterly* 25(3): 557–78.

Winton, A. (2004) 'Urban Violence: A Guide to the Literature', *Environment
and Urbanization* 16(2): 165–84.

World Bank (2000) *Cities in Transition*, Washington DC: World Bank.

Wright, L., and Montezuma, R. (2004) 'Reclaiming Public Space: The Economic, Environmental, and Social Impacts of Bogotá's Transformation',
Bogota: Human City Foundation.

Wright, R. (2002) 'Transnational Corporations and the Global Division of
Labour', in R.J. Johnston, P.J. Taylor and M.J. Watts (eds), *Geographies of
Global Change: Remapping the World*, Oxford: Blackwell.

Ya, Y., and Weliwita, A. (2007) 'The Urban Informal Economy – New Policy
Approaches', *Habitat Debate*, June: 4–5.

You, N. (2007) 'Sustainable for Whom? The Urban Millennium and Challenges
for Redefining the Global Development Planning Agenda', *City* 11(2):
214–20.

Young, I.M. (2000) 'A Critique of Integration as the Remedy for Segregation',
in D. Bell and A. Haddour (eds), *City Visions*, London: Longman.

Zaluar, (2006) 'Brazilian Drug Worlds and the Fate of Democracy', *Interventions*
7(3): 338–41.

Zetter, R. (2004) 'Market Enablement and the Urban Sector', in R. Zetter and
M. Hamza (eds), *Market Economy and Urban Change: Impacts on the Developing
World*, London: Earthscan.

Index